WALKING
<small>ON THE</small> GLASS
FLOOR

"Judy touches on all the key essentials of being a woman leader, but she does it by showing you who you are, unlocking your gifts, and setting you in your power. I love her direct approach. Reading her book is like having a conversation with your best friend over a cup of tea, only your best friend has years of experience and seems to know the truth and potential of your heart and soul and the precise steps to take. What more could you ask for?"

—FARZANA JAFFER JERAJ, Motivational Speaker and Best-Selling Author

"Judy doesn't simply write about what it's like to be a woman in a leadership role, she helps women develop the qualities they need to succeed in whatever roles they take on within an organization. In addition to being an easy read, Judy's experience guides readers to find their strengths and focus on what really matters ... the seven essential qualities."

—MELISSA KRIVACHEK, Radical Change Expert

"Judy addressing the topic of resilience for women in leadership is a five-star move. Resilience and courage to lead are essential skills for leaders at any organization that wants to retain staff, build a respectful workplace, and grow leaders from within. This is a must-read book for leaders and teams."

—CHARMAINE HAMMOND, CSP, Best-Selling Author and Speaker

"In *Walking on the Glass Floor: Seven Essential Qualities of Women Who Lead*, Judy Hoberman reminds readers of passion, authenticity, courage, and generosity—inherent feminine qualities that make women exceptional leaders. Judy showcases successful businesswomen and emphasizes ways in which our differences make us stronger. She also raises awareness of how women today can pave the way for emerging women leaders."

—DESIRÉE PATNO, CEO and President, NAWRB

"Judy knows firsthand what it means to be a woman in a very male-dominated industry. Judy's guidance is invaluable in helping women understand the importance of embracing and cultivating intrinsic skills to foster improved communication and collaboration in the workplace. In *Walking on the Glass Floor*, Judy covers this and much more. Of the seven leadership qualities featured in her book, my favorite is authenticity. Women need to embrace who they are and not try to fit into a mold in order to succeed."

—LIZ RICHARDS, CEO, MHEDA

"Ladies, it's time for us to lead! This book is a must read if you are in a leadership role or you hope to be someday. The seven qualities of a leader Judy addresses in this book are essential to making it big and making your mark on the glass ceiling or even better the glass floor!"

—JULI MCNEELY, President, McNeely Financial Services, Past President, NAIFA

SEVEN ESSENTIAL QUALITIES
OF WOMEN WHO LEAD

WALKING
ON THE GLASS
FLOOR

JUDY HOBERMAN
with STACEY STERN

WALKING ON THE GLASS FLOOR
PRESS

WALKING ON THE GLASS FLOOR PRESS
Southlake, TX 76092
www.walkingontheglassfloor.com

Judy Hoberman is Executive Director of Walking on the Glass Floor
Foundation and President of Selling In A Skirt. She is the author of
Selling In A Skirt, Famous Isn't Enough, and *Pure Wealth.*
www.walkingontheglassfloor.com

Stacey Stern is Connector of Dots & People at Stacey Stern Consulting.
www.staceystern.com

First edition published in 2018
Printed in the United States of America
Book and cover design by *the*BookDesigners
Photo by Debra Gloria Photography

Paperback ISBN: 978-0-9837885-6-0
eBook ISBN: 978-0-9837885-7-7

Publisher's Cataloging-in-Publication Data
Names: Hoberman, Judy, 1954-, author. | Stern, Stacey, 1966-, author. |
de Grosbois, Teresa, writer of foreword.
Title: Walking on the glass floor: seven essential qualities of women who lead
/ Judy Hoberman with Stacey Stern.
Description: Southlake, TX : Walking on the Glass Floor Press, 2018. |
Summary: This book by two seasoned businesswomen is for women who want
to cultivate and strengthen the seven essential leadership qualities of passion,
authenticity, courage, communication, decisiveness, resilience, and generosity.
Drawing from personal and professional experiences, it is filled with practical
guidance and actionable steps. With a foreword by Teresa de Grosbois.
Identifiers: LCCN 2017906024 | ISBN 978-0-9837885-6-0
Subjects: LCSH: Leadership in women. | Businesswomen. | Success in
business. | BISAC: BUSINESS & ECONOMICS / Entrepreneurship.
| BUSINESS & ECONOMICS / Leadership. | BUSINESS &
ECONOMICS / Personal success. | BUSINESS & ECONOMICS /
Women in business.
Classification: LCC HF5382.6.H6 | DDC 658.4/09082 — dc23
LC record available at http://lccn.loc.gov/2017906024

To my grandmother Sadie L. Flaum

CONTENTS

PART 3 Courage

PART 4 Communication

PART 5 Decisiveness

FOREWORD

"Grow a pair, Teresa."

The friendly mockery on Bob's face is clear. He's joking, and he's not.

I am literally the only person in the room with no balls. And everyone turns toward me.

It is 1989. This is the first project for which I have ever been given any real authority, and the operations engineer is running roughshod over me.

Sweat coats my hands. Survival thoughts race through my mind. My smile, plastered across my face, covers my shame. I decide right then that I must reinvent myself to thrive in this male-dominated organization.

Many women have had similar experiences. Difficult moments that convince us we have to be someone we are not to thrive in the corporate world. In fact, I spent years regaining my own authenticity after suppressing it during the early part of my career. I now realize and appreciate the ways in which my inherently feminine qualities help me excel as a leader and influencer.

When I first met Judy Hoberman and experienced her work, I could only say, "Eureka! She's found it!" At last, a philosophy and road map of leadership and influence that aligns with—and fully celebrates—core strengths of being a successful woman in business. These also happen to be qualities to develop if you have ever felt like a fish out of water in a leadership role. I suspect that, at one time or another, that includes most of us.

In a world increasingly connected through social media, we can put on our best face and present ourselves in whatever light we choose regardless of if that is who we truly are. But at what cost? How are you perceived when the real you inevitably emerges?

Authenticity in leadership functions similarly. We can act as if we possess the traits we think make a great leader, but if we are pretending, how well are we truly serving our colleagues and teams? Alternately, we can cultivate and strengthen our innate leadership qualities and genuine individuality. This is how we can show up as honest, vulnerable, empathetic, collaborative, and decisive women who genuinely lead well.

Passion is another quality that can't be faked. Have you ever taken a position or contract because you needed the work, but then struggled daily with the tasks at hand? Was it because you were unqualified, overqualified, or overworked? Was the job out of sync with your passions?

We all have financial responsibilities, and there may be times you choose to take a job because it provides much-needed income even though it's not aligned with your deepest professional desires. When that's the case, it is important to remind yourself of the value of that job so you don't stew in resentment. Yet the more you can lean toward what you are passionate about, the greater your potential will be to authentically lead and influence.

Judy's teachings provide a practical path to doing what you must while also exploring and moving toward what you love. Some days I feel undeserving of the privileges I enjoy as the head of a large, international organization of emerging thought leaders. Judy has helped me gain a fundamental understanding of how women sell and lead differently—and how we all can develop these gifts.

Whether you are an accomplished leader who wants to fine-tune your abilities, a young woman embarking on your career who wants to benefit from this wisdom from the start, or someone who wants to foster emerging leaders of any gender, *Walking on the Glass Floor* shows you the way.

—TERESA DE GROSBOIS
Author, *Mass Influence: The Habits of the Highly Influential*

ACKNOWLEDGMENTS

I am grateful to my grandmother Sadie L. Flaum for being the first woman who truly understood me and saw that I was intelligent and not "just" a pretty face. She never raised her voice, but she had a handy dishtowel that did all the talking. She was way ahead of her time.

Sadie lives on in her namesake, my first-born Stephanie, who keeps me on my toes and is a driving force for her generation. Stephanie is an ambitious woman in her own right, who also happens to be loving, generous, courageous, and resilient. She embodies the essential qualities of being a great leader, and I am so proud of her. When she was young and people compared her to me, she wrinkled that cute little nose and shook her defiant little head. As she got older, the head shaking side to side started to go up and down. Now, as I see more of me in her, I am pretty sure she is excited to see her in me.

Then there is the logical one, my son PJ. Without him I believe there were many cliffs I would have jumped off had his soothing voice and temperament not reeled me back in. He was there when I started my business and continues to support me whenever I need it. He knows what to say and more importantly what not to say. He truly "gets" me, and I know we would be great friends even if we weren't related. As his mom, I enjoy the added bonus of also having him as a great friend.

My husband aka the Colonel has been my number one cheerleader from the day we met. He pushes me to do things I otherwise would not have believed I could. Sometimes his simple comments spark a major project for me. This book and everything else it has inspired, including the Walking on the Glass Floor Foundation, resulted from his comments. He is the yang to my yin—the strategist to my implementer. I am grateful every day that this man chose me to join him on a journey at this stage in our lives.

This book would not have happened without my coauthor and editor Stacey Stern. The project blossomed into so much more than either of us initially envisioned when I asked if she could turn my radio show transcripts into a book on leadership. She poured over hundreds of pages of several years of radio show transcripts to distill the essence of my words. Blending my anecdotes and insights on leadership with her knowledge of the subject, Stacey created the book's structure and got to work writing about these essential qualities—always with you, the reader, in mind.

I love to write and share my thoughts, and sometimes I go off on different tangents. Stacey made sure that what I wanted from this book was and is exactly what I wanted AND so much more. She is my compass. Whenever I veered off course, she turned me around and got me back on track. It's funny how you meet people, and meeting Stacey was from a simple ask. You always hear, "Be careful what you wish for since it might come true." I wished for someone who would help me deliver something to you that authentically captures me. To my delight, Stacey appeared. I am forever grateful.

INTRODUCTION

My cheek is a scream of pain from where the hammer struck. It is an accident. My brother is horrified he hit me when I peered over his shoulder to watch him and my other brother learn how to build a go-cart. At five years old, this exciting afternoon with my brothers initially feels like a golden treat. Dad shooed me away once already with a firm, "Girls don't do things like this!" And yet, my inquisitiveness brought me back in and too close to the action. As pain radiates from my cheek, my father's words deliver a greater blow, "All you do is misbehave. You never listen and are more trouble than is necessary. Especially for a girl!" And with that, I am ushered away from the fun.

A wise woman told me to always look for the root cause of why we do what we do. Every story starts somewhere, and the day with the go-cart is where it all began for me. When I was growing up in the 1950s and 1960s, many young girls were told we weren't old enough or tall enough or smart enough to do even the smallest things.

Were you ever told you couldn't go on a ride at the amusement park because you weren't tall enough? Perhaps you couldn't go somewhere because you weren't old enough.

Maybe there was a teacher who didn't encourage you to join a special program because you weren't smart enough. Pairing "not enough" with "girls don't do things like this" is not a winning combination.

For much of my life, I thought of myself as a square peg in a round hole. I never truly fit in. My parents had one idea of who I was supposed to be, and I had other plans. Although I was not encouraged to follow my dreams, I absolutely was not to disrespect my elders. So I did what others thought I should ... until I couldn't any longer.

My saving grace was my grandmother Sadie L. Flaum. A true trailblazer for women and a fashionista, Sadie was a feminista ahead of her time. She always said, "Judy, follow your dreams and don't let anyone tell you that you can't do what you truly want to do. It may not happen today, but it will happen." She was right. It did happen, albeit fifty years later.

This book is about women in leadership. Moreover, it is about universal leadership qualities and was written specifically for women by women. While I typically talk, speak, and write about the differences between men and women, this book is different. It is about you and me and who we are as leaders—and who we can be. This book is for you whether you currently lead or want to lead a company, department, business, organization, or educational or governmental institution.

It is a practical guide to cultivating and strengthening seven essential qualities that will serve you well in business and life. Whether you are a seasoned leader or just beginning your career, *Walking on the Glass Floor* is for you.

Seven main parts introduce and individually feature seven leadership traits. Supporting chapters are filled with a blend of personal stories, sound advice, action steps, and exercises in the form of bulleted suggestions and questions for you to ponder, answer, and act upon. You likely will find it useful to keep a journal or electronic file handy to record your reflections and answers.

If there is a particular topic that calls to you, feel free to start there. For example, if you are feeling less than sure about yourself or a situation, you can head right to the section entitled "Courage." *Walking on the Glass Floor* has been designed so that each chapter can stand on its own. Alternately, if you read the book from start to finish, you will see that some stories and teachings build upon previous ones.

I encourage you to allow *Walking on the Glass Floor* to be a living tool. Keep it by your desk, bed, or in your favorite reading nook so it's handy to consult whenever you need guidance or inspiration. Underline passages that speak to you, make notes in it, and mark it up to your heart's desire.

As you periodically revisit this book, you may be pleased to discover that something you identified as a challenge or area for improvement a few weeks or months prior, now falls more often into the category of personal mastery. That certainly is my wish for you.

Speaking of wish fulfillment, let me tell you a story. In 2016 I decided that my wish or mission for the year was to help one woman a day reach her desired income and work-life balance, or to otherwise help her create an environment for success based on her own definition of success. My even bigger wish was to give women everywhere the tools they need to be successful in their careers, provide for their families, and have time to do what they truly desire with those they want to do it with.

I knew I had to start somewhere. So in 2016 I helped one woman a day. When I would mention my goal, I was often met with the response, "Can I be your woman today?"

Witnessing firsthand that so many women are looking for support and learning, I was determined to figure out how to provide that on a larger scale—and to take it a step further. In 2017 I decided that in addition to reaching more women, I wanted to contribute to charities they care about.

There are so many causes that matter to women. We probably all can name several organizations or non-profits that have made it to the limelight through great marketing efforts and healthy budgets. Other causes may be more local in nature and community-based. Individuals and businesses contribute to these causes, often without much fanfare.

Meanwhile, there are countless other worthy organizations getting off the ground and tirelessly striving to attract essential levels of support. Regardless of the size, age, or scale of these non-profits, the causes and goals they support are important to many women—and to our world. This matters to me. I wanted to come up with a way I could support causes other women were championing, but I wasn't quite sure how to go about it.

It was my husband, the Colonel, who envisioned linking the release of *Walking on the Glass Floor* to the creation of a foundation by the same name. He figured that if I could find creative ways to support women in leadership, both those currently in high-level positions and those developing themselves as leaders—as well as the causes that matter to them—it could and would be a movement in the making.

Soon thereafter, the Walking on the Glass Floor Foundation was born. Its stated purpose is: *To support and empower women by sourcing, publishing, and distributing educational materials for women in leadership and organizations that support women in leadership.*

Women are desperately needed and wanted at higher levels in companies, non-profit organizations, governmental institutions, new businesses, and on boards. More than simply a nice idea, our foundation is a collaboration of women and men supporting women regardless of age, culture, or industry. This IS going to be a movement.

Through the Walking on the Glass Floor Foundation, we also are developing partnerships with companies and organizations committed to women in leadership. This book is the first of many resources we are making available. Terrific programs are being developed as I write this, and mentoring and mastermind groups are being formed.

As a speaker and trainer, I work within numerous industries that seek to attract more women, retain them, and promote them into positions of leadership. Each year I see increasing numbers of "women's initiatives" being formed.

The Walking on the Glass Floor Foundation provides recommendations of vetted facilitators and consultants who offer current, relevant teachings. We reach out to other authors and coaches, and invite them to join with us as they share their expertise and brilliance with women in the workforce. Our online store includes books and other useful materials by various thought leaders.

As you read on, if you feel inspired to engage with the foundation either individually or perhaps via your company, there is more information in "Next Steps," the final chapter of this book.

Every day women worldwide accomplish amazing things. Surround yourself with those who do the right thing even when it's not in fashion. Reach out to those who generously share their knowledge and are aligned with your values. Support other women. Help each other.

You likely will recognize that many, if not all, of the leadership qualities in *Walking on the Glass Floor* already reside within you. Some may feel rustier than others. Perhaps, like many women, you have suppressed or hidden these gifts.

Consider this your invitation to reconnect with these seven essential leadership qualities. Cultivate and strengthen them. Bring them back out into the light and into the world.

PART I

PASSION

Passion. This beautiful and inspiring word has been bandied about quite a bit in recent years. You may feel as if everywhere you turn, someone is telling you to find your passion, work with your passion, or share your passion. Perhaps you have asked yourself, "What am I truly passionate about?" And if you do know, your next question may be, "Can I make a living doing that?"

Many people take a job or launch a business around an idea that excites them at the time or seems like a lucrative opportunity, but if they don't see an almost instant return, they lose interest. When was the last time you asked yourself, "Is this my passion? Do I love what I am building? Do I love it enough to continue doing this forever?"

We tend to be passionate about things we are good at; we enjoy activities that come naturally to us. But being passionate and skilled are not always enough to create a thriving business or become an accomplished leader. The most successful business owners and leaders take their passion and enhance it by continuing to learn and develop their strengths. To make any venture flourish, you must consistently move forward. This includes investing in yourself.

Passion can keep you energized and help you enjoy what you do. Since building a business or transforming a department or company requires a significant time commitment, this is critical. Passion is infectious. Potential investors and supporters can get swept up in your passion. Employees may be inspired to work harder on behalf of your espoused vision. Customers can share your excitement about a new product or service.

Passion also should breed patience and a willingness to endure. Patience enables you to see the big picture and make better decisions. But passion is not enough. If you are unable to use your skills or experience to build a profitable business, then you have a hobby, not a business.

When you work for yourself, you go from wearing one hat to wearing many hats. You need to know at least a little about a lot in order to succeed. You are now responsible for marketing, sales, accounting, maintenance, and everything in between. From when you wake up until you go to sleep, you may be thinking about your business: how to increase sales, how to increase income, how to get more done, how to handle challenges, how to get more time out of the day.

Several factors contribute to professional success. In addition to passion and ongoing personal and professional growth, essential components include a great idea, a great team, and great leadership. When properly channeled, passion can be the fuel that attracts investors, partners, and customers.

Do not lose the passion that brought you to the dance. That can happen when you are consumed with the day-to-day demands of running a business. If you find your spark fading, remind yourself why you started your business. Likely, you wanted to change something in the world. Go back and think about how you felt when you first decided to do it. Then, do it again.

When I worked in a corporate position, I treated that role as if it were my own business. While I did not have the same experience an entrepreneur or business owner would have and I didn't have to worry about finances or do everything myself, my mindset positively influenced the way I approached my job. By looking at my corporate role as if I was running my own business, I adopted a healthy CEO mentality of surrounding myself with terrific team members, making sure I modeled integrity and accountability, answering the tough questions, and creating systems to generate optimal solutions.

Whether you are the CEO of your company, the CEO of your own business, or an emerging leader in your company or field, your passion will shine through and the results may exceed your expectations.

Choose a job you love, and you will never
have to work a day in your life.
—Author Unknown

ONE

LIVE YOUR LIFE ON PURPOSE

Have you ever sat still, really still, and thought about what you are doing in your life and business? Do you feel fulfilled? Are you living your life on purpose? What does it mean to live on purpose?

At its simplest, purpose is what makes you … you. Some people seem to be born knowing their purpose, while for some of us, finding and refining our purpose can be an ongoing process. Either way, no one can choose your purpose for you. It is something you must choose or discover for yourself.

When I was younger, I decided, or rather it was decided for me, that I would be a teacher. In the 1970s women typically were teachers, secretaries, or nurses. Good girls did not disobey their parents' wishes.

I dutifully went to college, graduated with a degree in education, and became a teacher. Although I loved children, I knew being a teacher was not my purpose. How did I know? Well, even though I did not think in terms of purpose back then, I just never felt completely right or fulfilled. While I have the utmost respect for the teaching profession, I quickly determined it was not where I was supposed to be.

As it turned out, I did not even have to choose to leave that profession. There was a surplus of teachers at the time, and I was laid off. I was not so subtly nudged to discover my purpose—and that has been a decades-long process for me.

I moved from teaching to construction, and I held a host of other jobs before serendipitously landing in insurance. I stretched and grew there and felt like I found something exciting. Oh, did I mention that purpose is individualized? Most people do not consider insurance to be a sexy profession. Yet for me it clicked.

I began as a producer and rose through the ranks over many years, until I was an agency manager. Ready to try something new, I then spent a few years in Corporate America until a wise business coach guided me to start my own business.

I now feel as if I am living on purpose more than ever before. Without a doubt I know my purpose is to give women the tools they need to succeed in their careers, provide for their families, and have time to do what they truly desire. I do this every day through my business, Selling In A Skirt, where I coach and consult for women, do sales trainings and keynote speeches, and host a weekly radio show.

If I asked you to tell me what your purpose is, could you do that? Let's begin here. This is a good time to get out your journal or electronic file.

1. What and who matters most to you?

2. Where and with whom do you want to spend the majority of your time?

3. Do you dream of making a difference in the world? What does that look like for you? Be as specific as you can.

4. If someone were to describe you and introduce you to a large crowd, what would they say? For a moment, set aside your academic achievements and perhaps even some of your professional ones. What do you most want to be remembered for? What legacy do you want to leave for your family, community, or industry?

5. Other than your family, what brings you the most pride? What major goals loom ahead?

6. How will you accomplish them? What are you willing to do or not do?

7. Write your responses to these questions somewhere you will see them every day. Read them in the morning, at night, and in between appointments. Repetition is a great way to stay focused.

Some people are very intentional and live their lives on purpose. Others are not as aware and struggle to find purpose. Many simply respond to whatever life throws at them. Being clear about and connected to your purpose—even if it shifts and changes as you grow—provides you with a road map.

Each person has a unique journey and purpose.

Tell me, what is it you plan to do with your
one wild and precious life?
—Mary Oliver

TWO

DISCOVER YOUR TRUE CALLING

My true calling has always been related to women. I am drawn to help them succeed in business, ensure they have advantages and opportunities I did not have, and give them tools to succeed in their careers, provide for their families, and have time to do what they truly desire and deserve.

Are you wondering if you have discovered your true calling? Here are signs that you are still searching:

* You dream about being of service, making a difference, and doing something you love, but you have no clue what that might be.

* You feel as if something is missing, but you cannot quite put your finger on it.

* You feel anxious or restless, and you are not quite sure why.

* You are unhappy when the alarm clock goes off in the morning, even after eight hours of sleep.

* Everything feels hard. Nothing seems to flow.

* You find yourself asking questions like, "Is this all there is?"

* When people ask you what you love, you shrug your shoulders.

* Even if you know what you love, you make excuses for why you could never do what you love professionally.

* You dread talking about your work.

* You count the days until Friday and the months until your next vacation.

If this sounds familiar, do not be discouraged. Help is on the way! While you will not find your true calling in a manual, I will tell you what worked for me.

At my business coach's suggestion, I thought long and hard about this question, "If you could do anything and age, time, and money were not factors—and you could not fail—what would you be doing?"

This is not a question to answer in ten seconds. Since it could guide you to the next steps in your career, not to mention to deeper satisfaction in life, I encourage you to give it the thoughtful consideration it deserves.

Here are some other good questions to ponder.

1. What upsets you in the world and drives you to DO something?

2. Who are the people who inspire and uplift you? What are they focused on?

3. If you could take a college or professional course for free on any subject at all, what would it be?

4. In what ways are you drawn to help others?

5. Which situations in your life could be turned into learning opportunities for others?

6. What skill or talent do you wish you had and would be fun to pursue?

7. When you were a child, what did you love to do but later stopped doing?

8. What (or who) holds you back from pursuing what most excites you?

I know how daunting this process may seem. When I assign my clients these questions, I am sometimes met with a death stare. Yet my clients typically discover that while getting the answers on paper may be challenging, seeing them on paper is deeply rewarding. Celebrate that milestone!

Rest assured, there will be even more signs when you have identified and begun living in alignment with your true calling. Here are some clear signals you are well on your way:

* You are motivated and energized. You are increasingly driven to help others more than you are to simply complete tasks.

* You are ambitious. You do not feel comfortable when things stay the same for long.

* You love and believe in yourself.

* You no longer have the nagging feeling that "there is something more out there for me."

* You are not afraid to take risks. You realize that even if your endeavor fails, not trying at all is a greater risk—to your happiness, sense of purpose, and sense of self.

* You have experienced the joy that accompanies fulfilling work, and you know that returning to unfulfilling work is not an option.

* You surround yourself with others who are aligned with their calling.

You've got to find what you love ... Your work is going to fill a large part of your life, and the only way to be truly satisfied is to do what you believe is great work. And the only way to do great work is to love what you do. If you haven't found it yet, keep looking. Don't settle. As with all matters of the heart, you'll know when you find it. And, like any great relationship, it just gets better and better as the years roll on. So keep looking until you find it. Don't settle.

—Steve Jobs

THREE

HOW TO SPOT AN OPPORTUNITY

Some leaders have a natural talent for spotting opportunities. Other must hone this key skill. Do you readily recognize opportunities, especially when they do not show up neatly packaged? In the words of Thomas Edison, "Opportunity is missed by most people because it is dressed in overalls and looks like work."

About those overalls ...

Potential opportunities usually are not fully formed when you first hear about them. They often do not look perfect or shiny. In fact, you may see a lot of room for refinement and improvement. Yet there should be enough of a spark for you to begin thinking about and imagining possibilities.

Is this a business concept that makes a task faster and easier to accomplish? Is it driven by technology? Is it in an area you are knowledgeable, or more importantly, interested? You may be tempted to latch onto a hot, new idea, but if you need a team of people to explain it to you, perhaps it is not the best fit. However, if you truly believe in its merit and think you can learn what is necessary, then bring on an expert to evaluate and assess the opportunity.

Sometimes it is all about timing. Is now the right time? Both in terms of the time you can dedicate to this, and in terms of the viability of the product or service? Is the offering so far out there that no one seems to see or appreciate what you see (at least right now)?

Have you ever invested your time, energy, or money in something because you trusted the person behind it even if the idea seemed a little on the crazy side? If so, did it end up being a wise investment, or was it proven to be to good to be true? There are many things to take into consideration, and timing and intuition are big ones.

Your own clarity is key. Can you easily name the kind of opportunity you are seeking? Is it to make more money? Start a new career? Grow your tribe?

If you cannot precisely envision what you want, do not worry. Sometimes you must remain open and follow clues to hidden opportunities. Many years ago I was looking for a new career that would enable me to financially support my children and myself. But beyond that one clear goal, I could not identify, describe, or even name was I was seeking.

I never would have predicted that answering one particular newspaper ad would set me on a path to work in the insurance industry for the next twenty years of my life, then ultimately lead me to launch my company, Selling in A Skirt. I can guarantee you there was no giftwrapping involved! Now my business is bigger and better than I could have imagined, but I had to sort through a lot of coal to discover and create my diamond.

No matter how focused or determined we are, or how hard we work, it is important to remain humble and acknowledge that no one achieves greatness by herself. We need each other. I would not be where I am today without my business coach, Doreen Rainey, who also happened to be my first female mentor. Doreen helped me create my company, write a book, and develop the confidence to tell my story wherever I could. Although women often are reluctant to invest in themselves, I cannot recommend it highly enough.

At each step of the way, people will be your greatest sources of opportunity. If you are offering a product or service, asking the right questions and listening to the answers will lead you to the right people. Believing you are a valuable asset will make a huge difference in the opportunities you attract. So will focusing on creating opportunities for others. When you genuinely have someone else's best interest at heart, it comes back to you tenfold.

What if ONE opportunity could change your life?
—Marie Forleo

FOUR

COURSE CORRECTING

Life takes twists and turns. You occasionally may wonder, "How did I get here?" Despite your best intentions, circumstances can force you to reprioritize or otherwise change direction. Perhaps you chose to temporarily put your professional dreams on hold and take a job purely for the much-needed paycheck or health insurance.

But what happens if and when you decide to course correct? How do you initiate desired change?

Here are a few suggestions:

* Start slowly and see what feels right. There is no such thing as a perfect solution, so do not add undue pressure.

* Find someone who can guide and support you. Perhaps a mentor or a business or life coach.

* Identify your core values and clear out the rest. Name what you are seeking as well as your deal breakers.

* Consider choosing a lifestyle rather than a job title. Where and how do you want to live while you are "on the job" and when you are not? Do you want to be on the road a lot? Do you want to have set or variable hours? Would you prefer a

wide range of challenges or a clearly defined role? Some people choose the lifestyle and some choose the title. I choose what feels right for me at the time.

* Forget what everyone thinks and wants for you. My mom thought I would be an excellent teacher. Someone might think you would be the perfect engineer. Maybe you are destined to be a doctor or lawyer because everyone in your family is—and perhaps that truly is a great fit for you. The best thing you can do is follow your heart and take some risks. Staying in the safe zone will not get you closer to what is optimal for you.

* Be positive. Discovering your professional sweet spot begins with a positive mindset. If you want a solution, start looking for it. Realize it is a process. Despite the inevitable ups and downs, do your best to remain optimistic.

No matter how comfortable you are at your current job, at some point you have to be honest and decide if you are in the right business, position, company, or situation for you. Every quarter I go through my 3Rs, which stand for review, readjust, and release. I review everything I have done and am doing to assess if tweaks are needed. Then I readjust the things that have some speed bumps and try to make them run smoothly. The following quarter I review these adjustments to see how they played out. Finally, I release, which is the hardest part.

The release, if you allow it to, can make you feel like a failure. You may be releasing programs you built, trainings you designed, or articles you wrote for which there appear to be zero ROI. You may not even know why you did not receive a return on your investment. All you know is that you are wasting time and money, so it is time to release it.

To add levity while applying these needed course corrections, I like to shout out, "Plot twist!"

When obstacles arise, you change your direction to reach your goal; you do not change your decision to get there.
—Zig Ziglar

FIVE

MAINTAIN A POSITIVE MINDSET

Several years ago I was invited to be a guest on a radio show. It was my first radio show interview, and I was nervous. I had to drive to the station, put on headphones, talk into a microphone, and it was LIVE. On my way there, I wondered whether I would be able to draw from this experience going forward, or was it simply something I said yes to just because?

As I drove to the radio station, I challenged myself to decide whether my glass was half empty or half full. Should I turn around (which, admittedly, would not have been leadership-like), or should I forge ahead and march into the unknown?

I forged ahead. When I got to the studio, I listened carefully to the host's directions and advice. I was instructed to remove my bracelets and necklace so they did not rattle, speak slowly and directly into the microphone, and have fun. It sounded rather doable!

I was told I would be on the air for ten minutes. While I was waiting, I listened in to the guest before me who spoke not only for her ten minutes but also for eight-and-a-half of mine. The producer informed me I would have just ninety seconds to speak. After the show, he told me I said more in ninety seconds than other people say in ninety minutes, and he asked me back. After my next visit, I was offered my own radio show—and my radio career was born.

Meanwhile, I was given a recording of my first ninety seconds on air to use in my business, along with photos of me that I now use on my own radio show. If that were not enough, the sound engineer just happened to be someone with major connections that led to my first book signing at Barnes & Noble. My glass was more than half full, and I remain grateful I did not turn around during those fleeting moments of uncertainty.

Being a leader does not mean you are exempt from doubt or fear. You are human, after all. But leaders develop the discipline to manage their concerns and redirect to a grounded, positive mindset.

Here are some ways you can foster and maintain a positive mindset.

1. Reflect on your life. Is your life worth thirty minutes of quiet time every day? I would say so. Many people do this first thing in the morning, before getting on their computer or phone. Consider this part of your day as important as your most important meeting. You are meeting with the most important person in your life! Think about where you are, your potential, and whatever else sheds light on where you are heading. Let your imagination run as wild as it did when you were a child. Be open to your wisdom.

2. Incorporate daily affirmations. Create or collect inspiring messages to read each morning to align yourself with

positive outcomes. When my children were little, we had an Affirmation Jar, and each morning they would read one to start their day with an encouraging thought and a smile.

3. Do what motivates you. Find a few things that make you feel better and start doing them. I love music, and it definitely motivates me to start moving. This, in turn, inspires me to dance around the house, which puts me in a great mood and ready to tackle the day. Exercising on a regular basis can help keep you motivated and positive. You are doing something for yourself, and the results will be evident in more ways than one.

4. Visualize. Take time to imagine and actually feel yourself accomplishing what you want. Instead of casting it off to the future with "I will" or "I want," picture and sense exactly what you desire using the words "I am" and "I have." This is a powerful way to invite your dreams and goals into your life.

5. Speak with optimism. Do you ever mutter to yourself or even have a full-blown conversation with yourself that is anything but positive? If so, you must let go of those tired tapes running through your brain or that internal voice that brings you down. This applies equally to what you say out loud to others. Words do matter and once you say something, you cannot take it back. When someone asks how you are, do not be a Debbie Downer and give a long woe is me reply. Many years ago I rented office space from an amazing man. Each morning he walked around the building greeting everyone and asking how we were that day. Whenever someone asked him how he was, he would reply, "I am amazing." At first that struck me as odd, but I grew to appreciate that it was not only how he

started his day, it was also how he continued his day, and it defined how others thought of him. He was powerful in his own right as well as in terms of his positive impact on those around him.

I will leave you with this story about whether or not your glass is half full or half empty—or if that is even the most relevant thing to assess. I came across this on the Internet on a site called www.reachout.com, and the story attributed to "author unknown" is as follows.

A lecturer walked around a room while teaching stress management to an audience. As she raised a glass of water, everyone expected they would be asked the "half empty or half full" question. Instead, with a smile on her face, she inquired, "How heavy is this glass of water?" Answers called out ranged from eight ounces to twenty ounces.

She replied, "The absolute weight doesn't matter. It depends on how long I hold it. If I hold it for a minute, it is not a problem. If I hold it for an hour, I will have an ache in my arm. If I hold it for a day, my arm will feel numb and paralyzed. In each case, the weight of the glass does not change, but the longer I hold it, the heavier it becomes."

She continued, "The stresses and worries in life are like that glass of water. Think about them for a while and nothing happens. Think about them a bit longer and they begin to hurt. If you think about them all day long, you will feel paralyzed—incapable of doing anything."

That story made an impression on me. Perhaps it will help remind you to let go of your stresses. As early in the evening as you can, put your burdens down. Do not carry them through the evening and into the night. Remember to put the glass down!

> *A negative thinker sees the difficulty in every opportunity. A positive thinker sees an opportunity in every difficulty.*
> —Author Unknown

SIX

DREAM BIG

Some people think that dreaming big means you think too highly of yourself—that big dreams signal you are arrogant or perhaps directionless. But in truth, having big dreams means you are determined to live on purpose, are nurturing a vision, and are taking steps to make it happen. I encourage you to dream big. Otherwise, you will wake up to something smaller.

Imagine how different your life would be if you actively pursued even a few of the dreams you had when you were little. Life was simpler then, and dreaming was something we all did and were not afraid to share. As we grow up, some of us abandon our dreams while others stop dreaming altogether.

It all comes back to your mindset. Allowing yourself to be inspired and encouraged by your dreams can prompt you to set goals and establish an implementable plan of action. If you believe you can accomplish those big dreams, why not go after them? Why settle for the small ones instead?

I cannot imagine a world without dreamers. Without them, we would not have the things we take for granted like cars, phones, lights, airplanes, computers, and the ability to connect globally. Take a jog outside your comfort zone and surround yourself with other dreamers. Support each other.

Mentors can play a huge role in turning your dreams into reality. My mentors have helped me tremendously, and I am privileged to mentor others. What should you look for in a mentor? Someone who has expertise in your chosen area, wants to help you succeed, and will help you get there. In addition to listening to and guiding you, mentors will celebrate your successes with you and help you make adjustments when things go astray, which is inevitable when venturing into new terrain.

Here are a few more tips on dreaming big, setting goals, and achieving what you want.

1. Fear should not be an ingredient in dreaming big. We had no problem as little girls dreaming huge dreams because nothing was stopping us. As women in business, what is stopping us now? Set your goals and set your sites. Little girls with big dreams can become women with vision.

2. With your big dreams in front of you, make sure you identify the steps to get there. I always tell my clients to come up with a number (in terms of dollars, clients, applications, or whatever applies to them) they want to secure by a certain date. Then I tell them to work backward and break that number down into tiny little pieces to chart the steps to reach their goal. A dream written down with a date becomes a goal. A goal broken down into steps becomes a plan. A plan backed by action makes a dream come true ... and the cycle continues.

3. Track your progress. If you do not track your progress, how will you know when you have arrived? Make sure your starting point, goals, and milestones are clearly defined. No matter how often we hear, "Success is a journey, not a destination," I had to learn this the hard way. As a solopreneur, I thought, "Why do I need to do this? It is just me. I know what I want, so I will just go for it." Well that turned out to be one of the costliest mistakes I've made in business. You don't have to use an expensive program to track your progress. You could simply use a spreadsheet or piece of paper, but don't forego this important step. I ultimately rectified the problem two long, hard years after launching my business. I even wrote a book about all the mistakes I made, called *Famous Isn't Enough: Earning Your Fortune As An Entrepreneur*.

4. Do not do it alone, and do not let energy vampires suck you dry or feed you negativity. Surround yourself with people who believe in and support you. In addition to a coach or mentor, develop a network of colleagues who can be your accountability partners, just as you can be theirs. People can inspire you or drain you. Choose wisely.

5. Be open to failing. It is part of the process. When you dream big, you will have some hiccups. Brush off your bruised knees, pick yourself up, and continue on the path. The bigger the dream, the more steps you may need to take. Think of the forward and backward steps more as a cha-cha than as obstacles. When you realize that failing does not make you a failure, you free yourself to try many different things.

Believe in yourself and dream big. As you consider the path to take, do not forget about the rest of your life, especially your family. Work hard, take action, and keep pushing through when things get tough. Focus on the things that only you can do, and outsource the rest. Learn to say no, and most of all, dig in and stay committed.

If you don't build your dream, someone
will hire you to help build theirs.
—Tony Gaskins

SEVEN

BE A ROLE MODEL

The other day I was asked to name the most influential person was in my life. That was easy. It was my grandmother Sadie L. Flaum (and when you asked her name, the "L." was always included). Grandma Sadie told me I could be and do whatever I wanted, and it did not matter that I was a girl. Recently I was reflecting on the depth of her impact. Not only did she encourage me to follow my dreams, she inspired me to do the same for thousands of other women through my company, Selling In A Skirt.

In our celebrity-obsessed culture, it can be easy to lose perspective on what makes a positive role model. *Merriam-Webster* defines role model as "someone who another person admires and tries to be like; a person whose behavior in a particular role is imitated by others." While you may find you are drawn to different role models as you grow, I believe the best role models—and the best leaders for that matter—share fundamental attributes. Qualities that never go out of fashion such as: integrity, excellent listening skills, openness, confidence tempered with humility, passion, vision, talent, perseverance, resilience, ability to inspire, and generosity.

Some of us need search no further than our own families to find strong, positive role models. While other women might benefit from seeking role models at work, in their industry, or in the news. With the Internet, we can learn from and connect with inspiring women around the globe. Every day women are making tremendous strides in science, technology, finance, engineering, medicine, education, business, and entrepreneurship. There is no shortage of fascinating women.

Life is a constant give and take. Sometimes you will hunger for a role model, while at other times (or sometimes simultaneously) you will be a role model for others. When I was at the height of my career in the insurance industry, I was one of a handful of women in my company. I stood out. As I found my rhythm, I became a top producer, widened my network, and thrived in the business. This drew even more attention to me. If a woman applied for a position at my firm, I was the one she looked up to. If a woman was a single mother, as I was, I was the one she tried to mimic. If a woman was offered a promotion, I was the one she reached out to for "the real scoop."

Although I had not set out to be a role model, I became one. Was I perfect? No. But I always did my best, and I made a point to be available and accessible. I listened to, empathized with, and included other women. I supported them and encouraged their successes while remaining true to my values.

You may find it helpful to widen your lens when searching for a role model. There may not be one person who can meet all your needs. If you have multiple challenges, you may be best served by finding several people, each with their own expertise or niche.

Whether you are seeking one role model or several, here are some things to consider:

* Why do you believe you need a role model? What are you trying to learn? What skills and abilities are you seeking to replicate or master? While you may think it is a role model you are after, perhaps you need a mentor or business coach. To clarify, a role model may be someone you do not have personal access to. Perhaps someone you have seen on television, read about in the newspaper or online, or someone whose books you have read. In contrast, a coach or mentor is someone with a genuine personal interest in you. A mentor may or may not be paid, while a coach is a financial investment.

* What behaviors would you like to adjust or change? To supplement your self-assessment, get feedback from colleagues and clients.

* Look for role models who embody both the values and success you desire. Do they possess the leadership qualities I previously mentioned?

* Are you continually challenging yourself to grow in various ways?

Do not wait for the ideal role model or mentor to come along. Make sure you are always stretching yourself and learning. And be generous. Who knows, you may be the ideal role model another woman is seeking.

> *If you can't find a good role model, be one.*
> —Gale Ann Hurd

PART 2

AUTHENTICITY

My clients tell me they want to be authentic. Yet they often say they feel pressure to appear, dress, or behave like the seemingly successful women they see on social media, even though we all know that people only show on social media the version of themselves they want everyone to see. My clients also tell me they want the people they do business with to be authentic.

I define authenticity as being the real you. Sometimes people tell me they want to get to know me better. They want to know who I am when I am not on stage or doing my radio show. But I do not perform when I am on stage or on the air. I am simply me.

For some people, being authentic seems to be another job they create for themselves. Rather than showing their true self, they create a persona they think people want to see. I have been to conferences in which every single speaker seemed to have the same rags to riches story. Whether or not the stories were all true, the theme began to feel redundant.

We all have different personalities, challenges, and struggles. Each one of us must forge our own unique path to our definition of success. I believe those speakers would have come across as more authentic and original if they revealed their particular quirks along with the unique insights they experienced on their respective journeys.

Being authentic also means sharing what your audience needs and wants to hear at the appropriate time. Here is a perfect example. Speakers are storytellers who use stories to frame their teachings. Since the beginning of my sales career actually did begin with me climbing an actual ladder in a skirt, I typically tell that story. Part of it is funny, and part of it may seem unbelievable, but the entire story is true.

Once when I was the keynote speaker for a women's organization, I was prepared to begin with that story. But when I stepped onto the stage and looked at the audience of incredible professional women, I knew there was another story I needed to tell. It was about the moment my entire life and perspective on business changed based on a passing comment from a dear friend.

While I will share that comment and its impact in an upcoming chapter of this book, for now suffice it to say that when I revealed that pivotal experience to this room of more than one hundred and fifty women, everyone, including me, was in tears and shaking their heads in acknowledgement that this was exactly what they needed to hear. I felt completely exposed and entirely happy with my decision.

Each day we choose how we will respond to the invitation to be authentic. Being yourself and letting others see you is what it is all about.

Auditions are being held for you to be yourself.
Apply within.
—Author Unknown

EIGHT

WHAT DOES IT MEAN
TO BE AUTHENTIC?

Years ago I resigned from a high level, high-paying corporate job. That one decision opened the door to so many incredible opportunities I previously could not have imagined. The reason I jumped from that cushy place without a parachute was that I did not feel I could be my true self at work. It was reflected in the way I felt, the way I carried myself, and the way I was compromising on everything I believed in.

When I first entered the corporate side of insurance, I had grand expectations I would change the way things were done. I envisioned shaking up the system and shedding new light on the "it's always been done this way" mindset. I entered lofty corporate ranks with deep respect and support from insurance agents in the field who knew I had spent years proving myself as an agent.

I quickly discovered I was not similarly respected by those on the administrative side of corporate operations, mostly because they did not personally have a strong grasp of what actually happens in the field. Even though they paid lip service to treasuring the field agents, their actions did not match their words. I, and a few others, continually reminded them that the jobs they were privileged to hold directly resulted from the sales and hard work that the field agents did on behalf of the company every single day.

Having integrity means doing the right thing even when no one is watching, and that was not the norm inside that corporate office. The values clash felt like a tug-of-war. Things beyond my control were done that were not beneficial to my fellow agents. The situation became so stressful that I knew it was time for me to leave.

Sometimes I meet people who declare they are authentic, although they seem to be trying to convince themselves and others. Authenticity does not need to be announced. It speaks for itself. Being authentic means consistently showing up and behaving in accordance with our values and who we really are. That is no small matter.

Being authentic requires that we are introspective, self-aware, and honest. It asks that we accept our strengths as well as our limitations. Sometimes people with the best of intentions will challenge us. If someone believes you should do something they want you to do, but you know you have significant limitations in that area, you need to express this. To be clear, this is not about playing it safe or lacking confidence. What I am referring to here is about being aware of a legitimate limitation, owning it, and working with it.

Here is a personal example. I gave a keynote speech to several hundred women at a university. My talk was very well received. The person who invited me to speak held a top position at the university, and she asked me to return and speak to another group and teach them about ... are you ready? Social media. Those who know me well can attest that one of my greatest challenges is technology.

Sure, I can make my way around Facebook, LinkedIn, and Twitter. But am I qualified to speak to a group and train them on technical aspects and nuances of social media? No. When I told the dean I was not right for this task, she persisted. I was flattered. I tried to shift the topic to an area where I genuinely had expertise. Perhaps I could talk about the differences between men and women and how they use social media?

Remaining true to her needs and those of her students, the dean reiterated that she was seeking someone to specifically conduct social media training. I danced around the request until I realized that even if I tried to make this task fit me, it was too much of a stretch. I would not be able to deliver what this audience most needed.

In fairness to myself and others, I declined the dean's offer and instead gave her a referral. Grounded in her place of authenticity, the dean graciously accepted this. The immediate relief I felt confirmed this was the right choice for all involved.

Two common blocks to authenticity are fear of what others may think of you, or allowing yourself to get caught up in the expectations of others. If you frequently experience either of these, it may be time to surround yourself with people who love you for who you are, not who they want you to be.

I used to tell the insurance agents who worked with me to travel the high road at all times. Never be someone you are not, and never tell a story that isn't true just because you need to make a sale. Lies—even so-called little, white ones—will come back to bite you. When you tell the truth, the story is the story and you can't mess that up. People do business with those they like and trust. Being authentic gives you a leg up on your competition.

When you are authentic, you also have integrity. Who you are, what you do, what you say, and what you believe are all in alignment. You can trust yourself to make intelligent decisions when you are genuine and true to yourself. In turn, this leads to higher self-confidence and self-esteem.

Are you wondering if you need an authenticity tune-up? If so, here are some steps to take.

1. Revisit and redefine your values. The first step in behaving authentically is to know yourself, your values, and your desires. Are the values you grew up with the same values you now hold dear? When revisiting your values, do not be surprised if some of them seem to conflict. Work through the conflicts so you can see what feels most true for you today. Then make adjustments in your life accordingly.

2. Keep an open mind. Get rid of narrow thinking that might hold you back or cause you to be judgmental. Challenge yourself to look at all sides of a situation. Be open.

3. Be aware when you are being inauthentic. Are there times when you are being insincere? Do you behave in ways that are counter to your values? If so, why? Trust your gut. It

will tell you when you are off track and not being genuine. When your gut speaks, listen and adjust.

Only by being authentic can you realize your full potential.

Today you are You, that is truer than true.
There is no one alive who is Youer than You.
—Dr. Seuss

NINE

BE YOURSELF

How many times in your life have you been told to "just be yourself"? This can feel especially tricky when you are facing challenges while others seem to be passing you by with their successes. You may think, "Life would be easier if I were like _____." (Fill in the blank with whoever seems to have the most attractive life at that moment.) The truth is, the most common desire I hear from women in business is to be treated authentically by the people they work and play with.

Why are we not always comfortable in our own skin? For starters, there is no shortage of negative, critical, and judgmental messages aimed at women. When we turn on the television, read newspapers or magazines, or surf the Internet, we are bombarded with conflicting images and messages about our roles and values as women. Beginning as young girls, many of us create false, limiting beliefs about ourselves, which only become more complicated as we age.

To muddy these waters further, the people who know and love us may also encourage us to develop limiting beliefs. Not because they want us to be or have "less than," but because they may truly believe that by lowering our expectations or shrinking ourselves, we will be rewarded.

Here is one way this played out in my life. I was a single mother for almost two decades. My number one priority was my children, and I rarely dated. Well-meaning friends told me I was too picky to find a romantic partner. Many times I would see couples together and would think, "If I were more like her, I would have someone special in my life."

But I wasn't like the proverbial her. Although I didn't actually want to be someone else, it was hard not to wonder if my life would be easier or better if I were different. Until I decided that kind of thinking was not doing me any good.

Once I allowed myself to love and appreciate all of me, I began letting go of limiting beliefs. I am a strong, powerful businesswoman who acts with integrity. That doesn't mean I am everyone's cup of tea, though, and that is okay. When we are more ourselves, we may discourage relationships that aren't in alignment with us. This simply clears the way for those that are.

When I fully inhabited my own skin and my own life without excuses or reservations, I attracted the true love of my life. We are now married. I also left my corporate job, launched my own business, and am living with more joy and purpose than ever before.

How might you become more comfortable in your own skin? Here are a few ways.

1. Get in touch with your inner child. Most children do not care what other people think about them. They are generally happy and live in the present moment ... at least until they are taught to conform to the mold of familial or

societal expectations. Challenge yourself to shed the mold. Rediscover what makes you happy and do it.

2. Let go of limiting beliefs. Train yourself to become aware of negative thoughts that stream through your mind. Even those as seemingly harmless as "I'm tired" or "It's too cold to go outside today" or worse "I'm not successful enough to do that."

In my dating story, remember when I told you my friends insisted I was too picky? I decided to reframe that as, "I am selective. I am worth it." That made all the difference.

3. Follow your intuition. While life is not always a smooth ride, your intuition will help steer you in the direction that is best for you.

4. Relax. What's the worst that can happen? If you can, bring in some humor to take the edge off stressful situations. Let people see that you are human. Sometimes you can turn strained situations into something funny. It feels great to share a chuckle with others. Try taking yourself less seriously.

Here are additional benefits of being you.

1. You become a better listener. Instead of worrying about who you should be or what you should be doing, you can focus more on the present moment and the person speaking to you.

2. You will be appreciated more because you are not trying to get someone to see you in a different light. When you are being you, the other person sees the real you and doesn't worry that you are putting on an act.

3. You will be more relaxed. Trying to be someone you are not is exhausting. Being yourself takes no extra effort at all. Everything you do is real, and you cannot fake real. You are genuinely comfortable in your own skin, and it shows.

It takes courage to grow up and
become who you really are.
—e.e. cummings

TEN

BRING FEMININE QUALITIES
TO THE WORKPLACE

Some of the highlights of my insurance career were not what you might think. Yes, I was recognized and awarded by my peers, which was a goal. Yes, I wrote a ton of business, which helped thousands of clients receive proper protection in the event it was needed. And of course, being able to provide financially for myself and my children was significant.

But some of my favorite moments were when I saw my male coworkers' attitudes towards me shift as they really "got" the business value of my inherently feminine qualities. These revelations were particularly satisfying when they came from my manager who previously chided me for "being such a girl" and said, "Why can't you just get in, get out, and get the check?"

He initially was frustrated that I took time with my clients, asked them a lot of questions, and got to know them. He was concerned I was wasting time, wasn't focused enough, and would not succeed in sales.

Nothing could have been further from the truth. Precisely because I wasn't in a rush to "seal the deal," I earned my clients' trust and developed genuine, lasting relationships and deep referral networks. I approached each appointment "as if" I would have a new client. Even when I walked into a situation knowing they would not qualify for the insurance, I explained what I could offer and what their options might be with another company.

I ended up with more referrals from people I didn't sell to than anyone else. Why? Because I took the time to be present and answer their questions and concerns even though there was not immediately something in it for me.

This is one of the ways I approached my job and clients differently than my male counterparts. That is not to say they did not experience their own successes—of course many of them did—but there are inherently different aspects of doing business with a feminine versus masculine orientation.

Consumers tend to be savvier and more informed than ever before. You cannot hope you are smarter than they are and will dazzle them with your personality. We live in an increasingly relational world. As a broad generalization, men tend to be more transactional (get in, get out, get the check) and women are more relational.

In the world of sales, the goal is to get to the bottom line. Men may do so in bullet points or brief phrases that highlight the features of a particular product or program. I, like other women, tended to get there in a different way. I would establish rapport and begin building a trusting relationship before getting into the nuts and bolts. While my appointments might have taken longer because I asked a lot of questions, I also got my client's "why" in their own words, which helped me serve them better in both the short- and long-term.

Of course, the purpose of a sales appointment is to make a sale. Some customers prefer a more direct, linear way of communicating. It is essential to tune into the unique needs and preferences of your prospective clients. Do not make assumptions or barrel ahead with what you believe to be a one-size-fits-all approach to communicating. There is no such thing.

The very act of tuning into your client or customer by listening to your intuition is one way to bring feminine energy into your professional life. To elaborate, here are three tips.

1. Stop and breathe. Masculine energy is about moving toward a goal, preferably as quickly as possible. While of course you want to maintain forward momentum, if you spend all your time in that energy, you will burn out. This is where stopping, breathing, and taking time for yourself comes in. While you take a much-needed break to catch your breath, you can reassess if the direction you are heading is the direction you want to be heading.

2. Listen to your intuition. Many successful leaders, men and women alike, know that trusting their gut is one of their most important strengths. Some describe intuition as a woman's sixth sense. Unfortunately, we often are too busy to hear it or we do not trust it. When you take time to stop, breathe, and listen, you will get better at hearing your intuition. Over time, as you adhere to your intuition's guidance, you will learn to trust it.

3. Learn to receive. Feminine energy is about receiving, but that is not always easy for us. Many women tend to be more comfortable giving than receiving. This comes with great

risk. If you are unable to receive, how will you accept promotions or money and customers for your business? Leaders graciously receive.

I don't mind living in a man's world
as long as I can be a woman in it.
—Marilyn Monroe

ELEVEN

SHED OUTDATED STEREOTYPES

At a recent college reunion, my husband made a comment to an old friend that caught me off guard. He said I am the most intelligent person he knows. That is a mighty compliment, and I was flattered. But hearing him say that also made me uncomfortable, which was a huge "aha" for me that I am not immune to outdated stereotypes about being a woman.

When I was growing up, girls were supposed to be pretty but not too smart. My father regularly entered me into beauty pageants, and he took great pride in my appearance. It upset him when I un-entered myself. To him, I was just a pretty girl with nothing else to offer. I knew in my heart, though, I had a lot more to offer.

In school girls were told, "Don't let the other kids see how smart you really are. You don't want to make them feel bad about themselves." As we got older, the ante was upped when it came to boys. We were told to "dumb ourselves down" so we didn't scare away potential suitors.

Thankfully, times are changing and messages for girls continue to evolve. Today's girls and young women are hopefully being raised with far more encouraging messages regarding their intelligence and the myriad of ways to make positive contributions. There has been a push in recent years to attract girls to the STEM fields—science, technology, engineering, and math. A friend of mine runs a non-profit organization called Pretty Smart Girls, which means just that ... pretty smart. I love that.

Much room for improvement remains when it comes to incessant societal pressure for women to strive for elusive physical perfection. While "we have come a long way, baby" in some areas, we have a long way to go in others. Such as bridging the pay gap for men and women and securing harassment-free workplaces, for starters. But that's another book.

For now I will return to the college reunion. When my beloved husband praised my mind, a panicky version of a much younger self emerged from deep inside for a fleeting moment with this thought, "Don't say that to people I don't know. They will automatically judge me for having a brain and being female."

Yikes! Those old feelings from growing up and not letting people know you were smart were creeping in. Trust me, it lasted for just a few seconds, but that was long enough to realize how important it is to shed outdated stereotypes.

Today women bring phenomenal value to the business world. According to a publicly released study by Catalyst, a leading research and advisory organization working to advance women in business, "Companies with a higher representation of women in senior management positions financially outperform companies with proportionally fewer women at the top. These findings support the business case for diversity, which asserts companies that recruit, retain, and advance women will have a competitive advantage in the global marketplace."

Despite the facts, we still hear of people who are intimidated by truly smart women or women with ultra-dynamic personalities. To them I say, "If you are the smartest person in the room, you are in the wrong room." Surround yourself with bright, ambitious people to whom you can contribute and vice versa.

Let's acknowledge and celebrate all our strengths as women. And let's put tired, old stereotypes to rest once and for all. You are enough. The next time someone sings your praises, let it in and enjoy it.

After all those years as a woman hearing "not thin enough, not pretty enough, not smart enough, not this enough, not that enough," almost overnight I woke up one morning and thought, "I'm enough."
—Anna Quindlen

TWELVE

REMAIN TRUE TO YOUR BRAND

One of the most important things about starting or building a business is being memorable in a positive way. Why would someone want what you offer? Why should they seek you out or work with you? It usually is based on the perceived value of your products or services along with how they feel about you as a person and business-women. Are you honest, intelligent, and trustworthy? Are you capable of delivering as promised? Are you committed to delivering excellence?

The saying "you only get one chance to make a first impression" applies not only to what you wear and how you behave, but also to how your business presents itself. This is where your personal brand comes into play. Your personal brand allows clients to see what makes you unique and why you are ideal for your target audience. It may also illustrate how you and your competitors are yards apart.

When I started my company, Selling In A Skirt, I became a brand. As a business name, Selling In A Skirt said little and spoke volumes at the same time. At first, men would tell me they neither wore nor needed a skirt. Then I would explain that SKIRT is an acronym.

S = Standing Out
K = Keys to Success
I = Inspiration
R = Results
T = Time Management

My brand embodies the values I live and teach. Since most people associate the name with the article of clothing, I also wear my brand. As I mentioned, you and your business should show up as one and the same. For me, it is all about the SKIRT. I walk the walk and talk the talk. You will always find me wearing a skirt at professional events, and everything in my business is branded with the SKIRT philosophy.

To fully align your personal and professional brands, you first must know and be true to yourself. If you are seeking further clarity, begin by asking yourself, "What words describe me best?"

Think of three to five words. Then ask your friends, family, colleagues, and mentors to do the same. How do the lists compare? This simple exercise can be very telling.

If you are not thrilled with some of the words that came up, consider how you might address those aspects of your personality. If you are generally happy with what others have said about you, and if you believe it is an accurate reflection, choose the key words and aspects you want to incorporate into your brand.

As you build upon your personal qualities, consider your training and experience. What makes your offerings unique? What are your areas of expertise? What do you want to be known for? It is important to be as specific as you can without creating a niche that is so obscure that no one is looking for it. Typically, though, the narrower and more well-defined the niche, the more profitable it will be.

Consider how your brand fits in with your overall goals. Where do you see your business and yourself in two years, five years, and beyond? What are the vision and mission of your business? In what ways does your brand support and reflect those?

Next, let people know who you are and what you bring to the table. Do you love to write? If so, you can start a blog, write articles, or post thought-provoking questions on social media. You want to become "the" source that people turn to when they need information about what you are the expert in. You want to be known both offline and online.

You must be consistent, though. If you write or share something once in a blue moon, there is no guarantee your target audience will be around when it appears. Decide how often you will write, and schedule it so it continually goes out on a consistent basis. If you are technologically challenged, there are tools to assist you.

Be a guest on radio or television shows. I know many people are camera-shy, but I must admit, I think it is a blast. Before you jump onto a talk show or news program, try to get on the radio as a contributor on a topic in your niche.

I had the great fortune of working with a PR firm that consistently had me on Fox Business News as the Gender Expert, where I remain a frequent contributor. During some of my on-air interviews, I am asked, "How did you become a Gender Expert?" Although Fox gave me that title, it fit my brand. With each show, I reinforce my brand and my SKIRT philosophy.

How are you with public speaking? Go out there and share your message. I know many people who say they would rather have root canal than speak in front of an audience. But give it try. Perhaps begin with a Toastmasters course before moving on to Rotary Clubs and local Chambers of Commerce. These groups often need speakers, and you can gain public speaking experience while seeing how people react to the newest expert in town. When you are a more seasoned speaker, target larger associations and professional organizations. Public speaking is a great way to build your brand.

Finally, share your brand by networking. With many events to choose from, be strategic about where you choose to spend your time. Where are you most likely to find your target audience or strategic partners? When you share yourself and your brand with those who will benefit from it, you will reap rewards.

Everything worth having and doing takes time. Do not expect that just because you decided on your area of expertise, did a little networking, and wrote an article or two that you are suddenly going to be the "it" girl. Be patient. People listen and notice more than you may realize. I received an unexpected reminder of this a couple of years ago.

In the middle of the holiday rush, my local FedEx office was filled with customers mailing packages at the last minute.

My husband and I were there with cartons of books to ship to an upcoming conference. It was cold and icy, and I was wearing sweat pants, a heavy sweater, and a baseball hat. We planned to simply ship the books and return home.

Since I frequent this particular FedEx branch, I knew everyone behind the counter and they knew me. One of the young employees who saw us waiting, smiled at me and said in a booming voice, "Yo, selling in a skirt. Where's your skirt?"

Everyone turned to look at me. I responded, "I am just doing this one errand. I am not selling today." To which he replied, "Oh no, you told us we are selling every day."

Everyone giggled. Some nodded in agreement. I realized he had been listening and observing far more than I knew. It was a great lesson for me, and it was the last time I have gone out in public in anything other than a skirt.

Wear your brand, be your brand, and share your brand with everyone.

Your brand is what people say about you
when you're not in the room.
—Jeff Bezos

THIRTEEN

SOCIAL MEDIA, PUBLIC
RELATIONS, AND THE GENUINE YOU

Remaining true to yourself and your brand is especially important on social media. Many people view social media outlets as highly informal, "anything goes" gathering places. Doing so is not without consequences. Have you ever seen Facebook posts from a businesswoman and wondered, "What was she thinking? How can she post this when she has a business?" I am referring to certain personal photos, heat-of-the-moment tirades, or strong political or religious statements.

While I am all for personal expression and individuality—in fact, these are keys to authenticity—there is a place and time for everything. To lead in business, you need to demonstrate good judgment. Letting it all hang out is not the same as being honest.

Unless you maintain a small, selective Facebook page exclusively for close friends and family (or otherwise arrange your public and private settings accordingly), realize that the professional world will see and scrutinize your off-the-cuff comments as much if not more than your carefully crafted business marketing materials.

People want to know the real you. If they think your business brand is just an image, your business will suffer. To ensure that your public image accurately represents you, it must be consistent with your deepest values and personal sense of self. When you know and live in accordance with yourself, your professional persona will not feel like a mask you put on to go to work. Nor will it feel like something you need to escape from on social media or elsewhere.

There is still more to consider about social media and your professional image. How much should you publicly reveal about your business? Every business has its ups and downs. There is no need to vent or fret on social media if you are temporarily struggling with something. Do that privately with your mentors or business coach.

On the flip side, sharing great business news and successes can be fun. Just be truthful, grounded, and give credit where credit is due. Even if you follow these rules, realize a lot of people do not. To care of yourself, and do not compare yourself to others. When it comes to social media, you may be comparing yourself to a fabricated or highly exaggerated version of someone else's success.

All great leaders lead by example. By adhering to high standards of honesty and discernment in your social media interactions, you may encourage others to do the same. Still, it likely will take time for the social media tide of excessive self-promotion and oversharing to change. Accept social media for its gifts and limitations, and move on.

Perhaps your business is at a stage where you want to consider hiring a public relations firm to expand your reach beyond your current networks. As I mentioned, my relationship with a PR firm has been very fruitful.

If you want to hire a PR firm, here are two key things to consider:

* Trustworthiness. What is the firm's reputation? Who else do they represent? Are you a good fit for their areas of expertise and vice versa? If you choose to engage the firm, know you will be sharing sensitive business information. You will need to feel comfortable being totally up front with them so they can do the same for you.

* Chemistry. Do you feel you can build and nurture authentic relationships with and through this firm? Do you trust they will represent you, your brand, and your business with integrity?

No matter who you work with and whether you are in person or online, be the real you. Represent your business and yourself authentically, and align yourself with others who share your standards.

Make sure you deliver what you promise, and always treat others with respect. Be a role model and a thought leader. Authenticity is the business superpower we all can access.

> *Authenticity is not something we have or don't have. It's a practice—a conscious choice of how we want to live. Authenticity is a collection of choices that we have to make every day. It's about the choice to show up and be real. The choice to be honest. The choice to let our true selves be seen.*
> —Brené Brown

PART 3

COURAGE

A coaching client recently asked me, "How can I get the courage I need to move ahead?" As I considered her question, I wondered if she was using the word courage in place of the word help, as in, "How can I get the help I need to move ahead?" Or, was she referring to something deeper than that? Was she genuinely afraid she did not have the skills, abilities, or wherewithal to take the next step—that she was fundamentally not enough?

Whether we are accomplished leaders or moving in that direction, fear and self-doubt will occasionally emerge. Courage requires us to face our concerns, address them as best we can, then keep moving forward. We must mindfully keep putting one foot in front of the other.

When we are intently focused on the tasks in front of us, there may be no room to question whether or not we are in need of courage. In fact, until my client posed her question to me, I do not think I ever stopped to consider whether or not I was courageous.

Sure, I might describe myself as crazy, a risk-taker, daring, determined, or adventurous, but not courageous. It was an eye-opening moment for me to acknowledge that I have been quite courageous in my life—and to simultaneous recognize that courage is a cornerstone of effective leadership.

It was not until I plunged from my cushy corporate position into the world of entrepreneurship that people told me how brave I was. I am living proof of what I tell my coaching clients, "Often others see qualities in you before you see them in yourself."

Of course, courage is not a one-shot deal. We are presented with endless opportunities to be brave. My most recent challenge was, "How can I summon the courage to deliver a TEDx Talk that is both personal and valuable, and do it in a way that the audience can relate to?" I did so by working diligently on my speech, practicing it until I memorized it, refreshing my skills on working through the jitters, then getting on stage and delivering my speech.

If you would like to view my TEDx Talk, you will find it at www.sell-inginaskirt.com/videos. I invite your feedback, which also takes courage.

Courage is the commitment to begin
without any guarantee of success.
—Johann Wolfgang von Goethe

FOURTEEN

COURAGE IN THE FACE OF CHANGE

Change is inevitable. Sometimes change is forced upon us, while other times we initiate it. How skilled are you at handling the need to shift course, whether it is brought on by external or internal forces?

How do you tend to feel when you step outside your comfort zone? Exhilarated? Terrified? Lost? Remember, comfort zones are relative. Every time you step into uncharted territory, sooner or later you will find some degree of comfort there. Do not settle too deeply into this new comfort zone, as it may soon be time to step out again.

When you are in a leadership position, others look to you for cues as to how they, too, might manage shifting tides and forge bravely ahead. In case you need a psychological or confidence boost in the face of change, here are just a few of the benefits of change:

* Personal growth. Every time something changes, you have the opportunity to grow and learn not only about "things" but also about yourself.

WALKING ON THE GLASS FLOOR

* Flexibility. Change forces us to be flexible. You must bend and shift to meet new circumstances.

* Situations improve. It may not look that way at first, but it is up to you to optimize the situation. You probably did not choose to be worse off than before—at least not for the long haul. So whether the change was made by you, to you, or for you, get your big girl panties on and make improvements in your life.

* Your core values are tested and strengthened. No matter what comes your way, your core values are what define you, so look at change as a way to reinforce those values.

* You will become stronger. We all know the adage, "What doesn't kill you makes you stronger." I have found this to be true in my life. I also have learned that being stronger sometimes means asking for help.

* Opportunities will appear. They may be what you had hoped for, or they may be things you never previously considered. Be open and remain curious about what opportunities this change will bring.

While change can be difficult, not changing can be fatal. We probably all can name now-defunct businesses that did not adapt to the times or to changes in consumer preferences. This applies as much to people as it does to companies.

As Socrates (incidentally, not the renowned Greek philosopher but rather a character in Dan Millman's book, *Way of the Peaceful Warrior*) aptly advised, "The secret to change is to focus all of your energy, not on fighting the old, but on building the new."

Are you currently in a position in your career that you know is not right for you, but you are overwhelmed and fear that the unknown is more than you can handle? If not, do you know someone else in this situation?

Here are some steps to move through fear, overcome challenges (real or anticipated), and reach new goals:

* Brainstorm. What do you see yourself doing? Who are you doing it with? Do you know other people who created a company culture that inspires you? What do you want to eliminate going forward? Grab your journal or laptop and start writing down what you want your professional future to look like. Do not limit your ideas. Envision what you desire, and write as if that future is already here.

* Create a plan. You must have a plan, even if you are a solopreneur. Translate your list of ideas into concrete action steps. What are you going to do first? Who can you rely on to help you build what you want to build? Are you starting a business, or are you looking for a job? Write down everything in your plan.

* Start with baby steps. Rome wasn't built in a day and neither will your business or career. Start with one step, then add another. Do not try to do everything at once. You will become overwhelmed, and when that happens, nothing else happens. Prioritize what needs to get done and start there. When you complete one baby step, go for another one. Do not forget to take a moment and congratulate yourself on

a job well done. Throw in a reward or two and watch how quickly you move through your list.

* Take risks. Whether you are actively seeking a new job or starting a new business, you are going to need to take risks. Accept that you will need to leave your comfort zone to make new things happen.

* Get support. Do not do it alone. Surround yourself with positive people who can provide experience, wisdom, and connections. As Helen Keller said, "Alone we can do so little. Together we can do so much."

*Just when the caterpillar thought
the world was over, it became a butterfly.*
— English Proverb

FIFTEEN

NO RISK, NO REWARD

For some people the prospect of doing something risky can be daunting. Of course, it depends what that something is and what stakes are involved. Even so, the concept of risk may feel more approachable if we reframe it simply as "taking chances," which is something we all regularly do in life.

Here are some other ways to approach risk:

* Do not overestimate its size. Some of us tend to exaggerate potentially fearful situations. If that rings true for you, consider the possibility that what you face may not entail as great a risk as you might imagine. What benefits might it bring? Instead of thinking only about what could go wrong, challenge yourself to consider what might go right if you take this chance.

* Do not underestimate your ability to handle it. Some women frequently avoid taking chances because they second-guess their strength or ability to handle challenge. Do not allow yourself to fall prey to this version of self-doubt.

* Do not assume that if you do nothing things will get better. How many times have you gone through a situation using the ostrich theory? You know, if you stick your head in the sand, you will not see it, be part of it, or suffer any

consequences. I can tell you from experience that it does not work. Typically, if you do nothing, you get nothing.

* Be prepared to fail. Yes, you will fail and probably more than once. From each failure comes a lesson, and those lessons will bring you closer to success.

Since taking action can entail risk, asking yourself these three questions may help you assess whether you want to dive in or head for the hills.

1. What might I gain by taking this risk? Make a list of every happy outcome you can envision.

2. If I choose to take this risk, how and in what ways might this cost me? Consider a wide range of variables, including money, time, energy, your values, and relationships.

3. If I choose to NOT take this risk, how and in what ways might this cost me? Consider a wide range of variables, including money, time, energy, your values, and relationships.

While it is easy to say, "no risk, no reward," we all know that nothing in life is guaranteed. Even if you take a risk, there may not be an immediately obvious or sizeable reward. Of course, if you do not take the risk, there is zero chance of a reward.

So the question remains, do you move towards the risk or retreat?

Let's consider these benefits of taking risks:

* Taking risks opens you up to new challenges and opportunities. Start small and work your way up to something bigger.

* Taking risks broadens your horizons. You will leave your comfort zone and enter bold, new territory. Once you are there, you are on your way to even more opportunities.

* Taking risks sparks creativity. New situations will require you to open your mind and find new ways to solve problems.

* Taking risks can result in something truly amazing. Perhaps even well beyond your imaginings.

An interesting study by Mara Mather and Nichole R. Lighthall reveals as per its title, "Both Risk and Reward Are Processed Differently in Decisions Made Under Stress." Two consistent findings are, "First, acute stress enhances selection of previously rewarding outcomes but impairs avoidance of previously negative outcomes, possibly due to stress-induced changes in dopamine in reward-processing brain regions. Second, stress amplifies gender differences in strategies used during risky decisions, males taking more risk and females less risk under stress."

Men take more risk and women take less risk during stress? That caught my eye. The study goes on to explain that these gender differences in behavior are based on how our brains are wired differently, particularly in regions involved in computing risk and preparing to take action. Hmmmm.

Personally, I have started and re-started so many times that I cannot even remember all the chances I have taken along the way. Here are some of the biggies. I started a new career in the insurance industry at the age of forty knowing nothing about that particular industry. I came through the ranks of insurance agents as one of the only women, and I became an agency manager without ever having formal training or mentoring.

Our agency had no presence in North Carolina, and I was asked to build an agency there. For nearly a year, I traveled each week from Connecticut to North Carolina to establish an agency before moving there. Two years later I was asked to move to Dallas to take a corporate position building sales training, not knowing a soul there. I resigned from that big position to jump into the unknown again. I started my company, Selling In A Skirt, at the age of fifty-five and branched waaaay outside my comfort zone.

If I could do it all over, would I do it differently? No. Did I make mistakes? Definitely. Were the risks worth the rewards? Absolutely!

> *The biggest risk is not taking any risk. In a world*
> *that is changing really quickly, the only strategy that is*
> *guaranteed to fail is not taking risks.*
> —Mark Zuckerberg

SIXTEEN
MANAGE RISK

Every business faces risks that can threaten its success. Risk management focuses on identifying what could go wrong, evaluating which risks should be dealt with, and implementing strategies to deal with those risks. Businesses that identify as many risks as possible then strategize about how to deal with each one will be better prepared and have more cost-effective ways to address them.

As a leader, risk evaluation allows you to determine the significance of risks and decide whether to accept the specific risk or take action to prevent or minimize it. One way to evaluate risk is to determine the consequence of each risk. Many businesses find that assessing consequences and probability as high, medium, or low is adequate for their needs.

I find it useful to visualize and map out what is ahead of me. I urge you to consider creating your own risk map. This can be done with graphics and images, or simply with written lists. Using whatever format best suits you, plot the likelihood of a risk occurring and the significance of that risk to you and your business. You can assign each risk a value of one to ten, with ten representing significant risk. This helps you see how risks relate to one another, gauge their extent, and plan mitigating actions.

WALKING ON THE GLASS FLOOR

There are four ways to deal with risk. You can accept it, transfer it, reduce it, or eliminate it. For example, you may decide to accept a risk because the cost of completely eliminating it is too high. Or, you might decide to transfer the risk, which is typically done with insurance. Alternately, you may be able to reduce the risk by introducing new processes. Lastly, you may be able to completely eliminate that particular risk by changing the way you do business.

Here are some things to consider about risk management:

* Managing risk is as critical to your success as your business plan. Even solopreneurs need a business plan.

* Most entrepreneurs do not wisely manage risk. Instead, they gamble on success.

* Many companies fail or fold due to events they could have foreseen and prepared for but didn't.

* Do not become too attached to everything in your business plan. If something isn't working, let it go. If you need to refocus or pivot, do it. Expect to repeatedly jump into the unknown. Personally, I have my own 3Rs—review, readjust, and release. Can you guess which one takes the most courage?

* Have trusted advisors. When in doubt, turn to trustworthy colleagues, advisors, or mentors, or to your mastermind group or business coach.

* Be proactive.

In fact, "be proactive" is the first habit in Stephen Covey's book, *The 7 Habits of Highly Effective People*. It feels fitting to offer the following brief excerpt from his book.

Your life doesn't just "happen." Whether you know it or not, it is carefully designed by you. The choices, after all, are yours. You choose happiness. You choose sadness. You choose decisiveness. You choose ambivalence. You choose success. You choose failure. You choose courage. You choose fear. Just remember that every moment, every situation, provides a new choice. And in doing so, it gives you a perfect opportunity to do things differently to produce more positive results.
—Stephen Covey

SEVENTEEN

CONQUER FEAR

When we look at the people we work with or others in our industry, we occasionally may consider how lucky they are, how easily things come to them, and how they or their business became a household name overnight. In all likelihood, none of that is true.

Every person who experiences success, has also seen their share of failures. But those who are serially successful learn from their failures, figure out how to overcome them, and conquer their fears so they can apply what they learn and try again.

There is a difference between managing or optimizing risk as we just discussed, and allowing fear to take over and lead to self-sabotage. Just as we need to learn to deal with legitimate failure—we gave it our best shot, but the business was not viable—we also need to manage fear.

Consider the following:

* Regret is worse than failing. While failing is not fun, there is nothing worse than having regrets, especially of the "should've, could've, would've, if only" variety. Take the chance. If you fail, you can start again. In the end, we most regret the chances we didn't take.

* Identify the root cause of your fear. When you do, you can acknowledge it then overcome it. Have you considered that everything you desire may be on the other side of fear?

* Many times we set lofty goals then overwhelm ourselves or quit before we even begin. Break your goals down into small pieces. Take baby steps.

* Prioritize and stop procrastinating. When we aren't certain how to begin, we may start filling our day with busywork. Busywork does not move your business forward. To the contrary, it can be demotivating and contribute to self-doubt. Write out your list, prioritize, and get the most important things done first. When you prioritize, the significant things get done.

* Trust your gut. You know what you need to do. You know what is right. I bet if you look back at what has worked for you and what has not, most of the failures arose when you did not trust yourself. Always trust your gut. It knows what your head has not yet figured out.

Many of our fears, or at least the flavor or essence of them, are similar to fears we had as children. How would you guide a child to face his or her fears?

Here are some of my suggestions.

1. Write down your fears. Think about them carefully and be honest with yourself. Whether you are afraid of clowns, giving a presentation, public speaking, or succeeding, get the list going.

2. Next to each fear, write down at least one reason not to fear this item. Then write down at least one action step you can take to move beyond that fear. For example, if you are afraid of public speaking, perhaps begin by doing a short practice speech in front of the mirror or with your children, a friend, or even your pets.

3. When you are in a situation and feel fear coming on, breathe! Take several deep, slow breaths. Then take out your list. Read what you wrote to remind yourself why the fear is unfounded and how to move past this state. Breathe some more.

4. Face your fears directly. Do the things you are afraid to do so you can cross them off your list. Sign up to speak at a small group gathering. Even though you may be nervous, you will get through it. You may even discover it was easier or more rewarding than you anticipated. Even if you choose not to do it again, you can take pride in facing your fear and surviving.

5. Focus on this moment. Fear is often the result of our mind not focusing on the here and now. The past is done. Obsessively rehashing old concerns is unproductive. The future is not here yet. Imagining worst-case scenarios is similarly unproductive. I love the saying, "Yesterday is history, tomorrow is a mystery. Today is a gift, that's why they call it the present."

I want to circle back to my earlier comment about becoming a household name overnight. Those "overnight sensations" were almost always many years in the making. Ask any one of them. If they are honest, they will tell you about the fears they faced, how they conquered them, the failures they experienced, and how courage, persistence, and resilience contributed to their success.

> *You gain strength, courage, and confidence by every*
> *experience in which you stop to look fear in the face.*
> *… You must do the thing you think you cannot do.*
> —Eleanor Roosevelt

EIGHTEEN

CULTIVATE CONFIDENCE

Self-confidence often is a differentiator between people who achieve their goals versus those who do not. You must know yourself, grow yourself, and believe in yourself to be an effective leader and businesswoman.

Economies go up and down, technology is constantly changing, markets shift, and new competitors come along. While we all face challenges, an accurate yet healthy sense of yourself can help you get through the tough times.

When I think about self-confidence, I always come back to intelligence. Sure, you can walk into a room with your head held high and your posture erect, but ultimately what impresses is what you have to say and how you converse on a multitude of topics. Knowledge is power, and through that power comes confidence.

I don't know about you, but sometimes I find myself wondering what others might think about what I have said or done. As soon as I notice that, I try to make sure I don't head down the slippery slope of "not enough" that plagues so many women. You know, I am not successful enough, strong enough, tall enough, rich enough, pretty enough, and perhaps even smart enough. Then I course correct my attitude. I remind myself that sharing knowledge often helps others. It also can be a vehicle for my confidence to shine and a reminder that I am always more than enough.

Several years ago I decided to put together a telesummit and identified twenty-three women I wanted to invite. I would be the twenty-fourth. The e-mails were ready to go when I told my husband I decided not to send them. I was going to cancel the event before it began. With a look of surprise, he asked, "Why?"

I told him I was not famous enough or smart enough. Then I threw in tall enough. Although my height is irrelevant, it felt right in the moment. He reminded me who I am, what I stand for, and that people are attracted to me because of my integrity, reputation, value, and, yes, humor.

I said I would think about it, and I gave myself until 6 p.m. that evening to either hit send or delete on my e-mail invitations. You can guess which direction I was heading. At 5:59 p.m. I hit send and immediately turned off my computer. I did not want to read the reasons why they would all say no. I did not sleep well that night for fear that at 6 a.m. I would have to suffer through twenty-three no's and accept it.

At promptly 6 a.m. I opened my computer to see that twenty-two of the twenty-three replied with, "Absolutely!", "What do you need?", "What can I do?", "Thank you for including me!", and so on. The twenty-third responded similarly about an hour later (she was on a different continent) and was as excited as the rest. I reflect on this story when I need to banish worries about being enough.

Here are additional ways to build or increase your self-confidence:

* Understand your strengths and weaknesses. Do what you are good at because that is where you will shine. Continue to cultivate and expand upon your strengths. Understand your weaknesses so no one can use them against you. Delegate tasks that are not your strengths, and concentrate on what you do best.

* Devise a strategy to help you achieve your goals. Be crystal clear and detailed in your focus. Our time is precious. Everyone has the same amount each day, yet some people complete what they set out to do while others do not. When you fail to plan, you are planning to fail.

* Be accountable. No one can do it alone. Have an accountability partner or become one. Consider investing in a business coach.

* Before a big meeting, presentation, or public speaking engagement, listen to an inspiring song, recite an affirmation, wear something that makes you feel good, or give yourself a pep talk. It might be something as simple as "you've got this!" before you step out into the spotlight.

* Decide how you can make a difference. You do not have to donate millions of dollars to have an impact. Can you mentor young women? Become a Big Sister for someone lacking in role models? Volunteer at a local retirement community, or perhaps serve meals to the homeless?

When I consider how my professional life has unfolded, I always think about what brought me to the dance and who took me for a spin on the dance floor. In other words, who paved the way for me? That is where I believe some of my courage initially emerged.

As I previously mentioned, for many years I was either the only woman or one of just a few women in my workplace. I never had a female coworker in a position senior to me nor did I have any who were my peers. As the most senior woman in the office, I had to create my own playbook. While I was fortunate to have great male mentors who shared their experience and expertise, I longed to have a female mentor.

Never forgetting where I came from, when I launched my own business, I aimed to be that person for other women. Knowing that most businesses fail within their first five years, I knew I had to make my business profitable AND that I would mentor young women. That was how I most wanted to give back and make a true difference.

My first young mentee came to me when her male mentor asked if I had any interest in mentoring her. It was like music to my ears. I jumped at the opportunity. I met my next two mentees at networking events. Both were looking for a female role model with business experience. As the saying goes, "When the student is ready, the teacher appears."

As luck or destiny would have it, I was exactly who they were seeking. My next mentee and I were matched up through a university program. Although our majors could not have been more different, there was pure magic in the way we meshed.

When my husband and I got married, all of my mentees were there, and I introduced them as my bonus daughters. Each one is completely different from the others yet they share tremendous respect and affection for one another.

One of my mentees recently got engaged, one got married, one had her first child, and one just received a fabulous promotion. While the credit for their successes is all theirs, I know we have positively impacted one another.

The best way to get approval is not to need it.
—Hugh MacLeod

NINETEEN

WILL YOU CHANGE THE WORLD?

Every day you make decisions about the life you want to lead. Perhaps you are working toward a promotion or starting your own business. You want to bring value to those around you. You may even want to change the world.

How do we do that? Some may say it takes a lot of money or power. To that I say, HA! You can change at least a piece of the world by giving someone your time, smiling at them, or even paying them a compliment.

Every day I compliment someone I don't know, whether it's about what they are doing, what they are wearing, or why I am drawn to them. Sometimes they respond with a simple thank you, sometimes with a look of shock, and sometimes there is no reaction. I know there are people who are seldom complimented, and my words may bring them some joy.

Recently I was at breakfast and two older women were sitting at a nearby table. One woman looked very unhappy and did not smile at all. The other was trying to engage her in conversation and did not seem to be successful. I said to the friend I was with that the woman who wasn't smiling was beautiful and I was going to tell her that. And I did. She had a sparkle in her eyes when I told her and she put her hand on mine and said, "Thank you. You made my day."

Who do you think felt better about our exchange? While I may have helped change her world for at least that moment, she did even more for me.

What does it take to change the world on a larger scale? Influence. According to *Merriam-Webster,* influence is "the power to change or affect someone or something; the power to cause changes without directly forcing them to happen; a person or thing that affects someone or something in an important way." Isn't this what leaders, entrepreneurs, and business owners want to do?

As an influencer, you likely will want to help others become influential as well. While there are all kinds of people who make difference, I most respect those who care about and support others. Whose efforts expand far beyond their immediate self-interest. Those are the people who truly change the world for the better.

Here are ten remarkable women who exerted their influence to make the world a better, kinder place. Many of them faced challenges and injustices that hopefully you and I will never have to endure—and, in many cases, we have them to thank for that.

While most of these women lived or live in different times and places than you and I, they are united by their ability to overcome adversity and make our world a better place.

1. Susan B. Anthony became an advocate for women's suffrage, women's property rights, and the abolition of slavery. Anthony tried to vote in the 1872 presidential election to challenge suffrage. While Anthony was never able to legally

vote, the 19th amendment, ratified in 1920, was named the "Susan B. Anthony Amendment."

2. Dr. Elizabeth Blackwell was the first woman to receive a medical degree from an American medical school. She first overcame numerous odds, including gaining admittance to an all-male institution and personally financing her medical school education. Along with two other female doctors, Dr. Marie Zakrzewska and her sister Emily, Dr. Blackwell opened the New York Infirmary for Women and Children in 1856. The following year they added a medical college to provide more opportunities for women doctors and to provide specialized medical care for those who otherwise could not afford it.

3. Marie Curie was the first person to win two Nobel Prizes. The first prize was in physics in 1903, with her husband, Pierre Curie, and Henri Becquerel for their study in spontaneous radiation. The second prize was in chemistry in 1911 for her work in radioactivity. She also became the first woman professor of general physics in the faculty of sciences at the Sorbonne in 1906. She had master's degrees in both physics and mathematical sciences, and was the first woman to obtain a doctor of science degree.

4. Mother Teresa was a Catholic nun who was canonized (recognized by the church as a saint) on September 4, 2016, nineteen years after her death. Although she spent the majority of her life in India, her international charity work included helping evacuate hospital patients in war-torn Lebanon, providing earthquake relief in Armenia, and ministering to famine victims in Ethiopia. In 1950 she founded the Missionaries of Charity, a Roman Catholic congregation

of sisters worldwide who vowed to give "wholehearted free service to the poorest of the poor." Among her many honors was the Nobel Peace Prize, which she was awarded in 1979 "for work undertaken in the struggle to overcome poverty and distress, which also constitutes a threat to peace."

5. Anne Frank was a diarist, writer, and one of the most recognized Jewish victims of the Holocaust. Her posthumously published wartime diary, *The Diary of a Young Girl*, quickly became a classic. Born in Frankfurt, her family moved to Amsterdam when she was four due to widespread anti-Semitism in Germany. When the Nazis occupied the Netherlands in 1940, she and her family spent two years hiding in an annex. The family was ultimately discovered and sent to concentration camps. Anne died at the age of fifteen just weeks before the war ended.

6. Ellen Johnson-Sirleaf was the first elected female head of state in Africa when she took office as the president of Liberia in January 2006. She signed a freedom of information bill and made reduction of the national debt a cornerstone of her presidency. She established a truth and reconciliation commission and became a global icon with her commitment to fighting dictators, corruption, and poverty through empowerment of women and girls. She and two other female leaders, Leymah Gbowee and Tawakkol Karman, were awarded the 2011 Nobel Peace prize for their nonviolent role in promoting peace, democracy, and gender equality.

7. Shirin Ebadi is an Iranian lawyer, human rights activist, and the first female judge in Iran. After Khomeini's revolution in 1979, she was dismissed as a judge. She then opened

a legal practice to defend people being persecuted by the authorities. She was imprisoned in 2000 for criticizing her country's hierocracy. She won the 2003 Nobel Peace Prize for her pioneering efforts for democracy and human rights, especially those of women, children, and refugees. She is the first Iranian and first Muslim woman to win the prize.

8. Benazir Bhutto was a political activist from a young age. In 1984 she founded an underground organization to resist the military dictatorship in Pakistan. In 1988 she became prime minister at only thirty-five years old, making her one of the youngest chief executives in the world. She was the first woman to head a Muslim majority nation, and the only one to head it twice. She was assassinated in 2007 while leaving a campaign rally. Her efforts to promote democracy and women's empowerment are an important part of her legacy.

9. Dr. Mae Jemison, an American physician, is the first African-American female astronaut. Before her career at NASA, she worked in a Cambodian refugee camp in Thailand and served in the Peace Corps in Sierra Leone and Liberia. She was accepted to NASA's astronaut training program in 1987. As a science mission specialist aboard the Space Shuttle Endeavour in 1992, she became the first African-American woman in space.

10. Malala Yousafzai is a Pakistani advocate for girls' education and the youngest-ever Nobel Prize winner. When Malala was just eleven years old, she began blogging about life under the Taliban, speaking out directly against their threats to close girls' schools. In October 2012 a gunman shot her and two other girls as they were coming home from

school. Malala survived the attack and in 2013 published an autobiography, *I Am Malala: The Girl Who Stood Up for Education and Was Shot by the Taliban*. In October 2014 she received the Nobel Peace Prize along with Indian children's rights activist Kailash Satyarthi.

We all can make a difference. We each have special gifts and a unique path.

While you may or may not impact the world as dramatically as these girls and women have, there is important work for you to do.

In case you are wondering how to take the next step, here are a few ideas to help you get started:

* What issues do you really care about? What problem or problems do you want to address? Are they local, national, or global in scope?

* Find out who and what groups have organized around the issue or issues that matter most to you. Thanks to the Internet, it will not take long to discover this.

* Choose an organization or organizations to get involved with. Then join and take action. If the group is near you, show up! Attend the meetings, volunteer, and get involved. See what they most need and how that best matches your skills and abilities. If the organization is based elsewhere, find out how to plug into their virtual operations. Perhaps they need someone to set up an on-the-ground presence in your community, state, or region.

* If you are not sure what really calls to you, read the newspaper and follow the news to see what sparks you. Consider what issues and causes mattered to you as a child and what you hold dear now. Oftentimes our deepest values and passions are related.

* Do you want to play big or small? There is no right answer. As I said, we each have our own path and gifts. In any event, it is okay to start small and grow from there.

* In your own words, what does it mean to change the world? Real change comes from within. Do you want to start with your interior world (yourself?), your family unit, or beyond?

Go into the world and do well. But more importantly, go into the world and do good.
—Minor Myers, Jr.

PART 4

COMMUNICATION

Clear, thoughtful communication is a cornerstone of a healthy workplace. How we speak, listen, ask questions, write, and otherwise convey our ideas and execute our plans can significantly impact our success or lack thereof. Sometimes what you say is not heard the way you intended it, and sometimes what you want to say does not translate well when you write it.

As a leader, in addition to cultivating your own communication skills, you must want to understand how your team, your department, and your peers communicate. What are their preferred methods? Are those yours? I have found that many women prefer to speak to someone or meet in person rather than send e-mails or texts.

For me, receiving a text from someone I don't know is the quickest way to lose me. Relying almost exclusively on e-mails or texting can be problematic since tone and nuance can be difficult to discern. When multiple e-mails are sent back and forth without any spoken exchanges, confusion can reign.

Case in point. I was in the process of completing a project. My manager and I were going back and forth via e-mail about specific modifications and refinements. This chain of communication began at 8 p.m. By 11 p.m. the e-mails were getting shorter and the tone had shifted.

We both were tired and guess who overlooked one of the e-mails. Yes, that would be me. I responded to one, missed another, and then responded to the next one. Her subsequent reply was less than pleasant. To me, it felt accusatory rather than constructive. I e-mailed something back, then she did, and then we agreed we no longer would e-mail one another after 8 p.m. since we lost the quality and clarity of communication we both desired.

At its core, communication is about doing our best to understand one another. Put yourself in someone else's shoes and try to receive what you are saying in the way you are saying it. I often suggest to my clients that they speak their presentations and important conversations out loud to themselves before presenting them to others. This can be a powerful way to talk, listen, and learn.

Speak in such a way that others love to listen to you.
Listen in such a way that others love to speak to you.
—Author Unknown

TWENTY

FOSTER HEALTHY RELATIONSHIPS

According to the Center for Creative Leadership, people who have the ability to build and maintain strong, lasting relationships are more effective and achieve greater success than those who ignore or struggle with this competency. While there are still women who believe they need to do it all and be everything to everyone, more and more women are hanging up their Superwoman capes and creating relationships with men and women who can assist them, introduce them to others in their circles, and create new opportunities.

In today's world, every business is a relationship business. Everything we do depends upon the relationships we develop both in person and online with customers, coworkers, vendors, supervisors, employees, partners, and competitors.

Even when we recognize the importance of healthy relationships, will we always be successful in this regard? No. Despite good intentions, relationships don't always gel. Common reasons include unmet expectations, unfilled commitments, personality conflicts, and poor communication.

Being a clear, effective communicator is an essential leadership skill, as we will explore throughout this chapter. Developing awareness of yourself and others are related competencies. The most accomplished leaders know how to shine the light on others and tend well to their needs.

Here are some suggestions for building and nurturing your business relationships:

* Be authentic. Know yourself and represent yourself honestly.

* Invest in other people's success. Seek to understand what they need and how you can support them.

* Listen with an open mind and heart. Give the other person your full attention and try to hear not only their words, but also their emotions, concerns, fears, and insights.

* Focus on WE. Move from "I have all the answers" to "Let's create solutions together."

* Don't keep score. Pettiness doesn't serve.

* Do what you say you will do. Follow through. Be consistent.

* Share information. Be generous in your communications. Keep others informed of changes that may impact them and their expectations.

* Model honesty and accountability. If you make a mistake or misjudgment, admit it quickly and provide a remedy.

* Give feedback that creates value. If you don't agree with how something is being handled, don't be a "yes" person. Share your thoughts constructively to open up possibilities.

* Receive feedback graciously.

* Appreciate others. Look for what others are doing well and tell them. Relationships should be fun, even in a professional setting.

* Stay connected. It takes time and consistency to build trust and relationships.

Since establishing rapport and staying connected are essential to fostering healthy relationships, the following suggestions relate to timely, meaningful ways to stay in touch.

1. Follow up on meetings promptly with an e-mail. While a meeting is fresh in your mind, send an e-mail to let the person know you enjoyed meeting them and why. You may want to reference something they said that stood out. If you promised to send them something, do it before the end of the day.

2. Pick up the phone. Making and receiving phone calls can be a refreshing change from text messaging and other digital communication. In contrast to texts and e-mail, it is typically much easier to decipher tone and intent when you are speaking directly with someone.

3. When the shoe is on the other foot and someone calls you, return their call promptly. It does not have to be within seconds, but it should be within the day.

4. If you want to stand out from the crowd, send a handwritten note. In fact, if you are lucky enough to mentor a young man or woman, get them in the habit of doing that from the

start. They might grumble a bit at first, but they will thank you for it in the long run.

No one can copy the relationships you build with your customers, clients, and colleagues. While others may have similar access to competitive intelligence, no one can replicate the rapport you create.

A great relationship is about two things.
First, find out the similarities. Second, respect the differences.
—Author Unknown

TWENTY-ONE

CREATE AN ENVIRONMENT
FOR GREATNESS

While you cannot order greatness, you can create an environment where greatness occurs.

This begins with assessing and understanding how your employees and coworkers define greatness for themselves and how they believe they can best contribute.

What makes their brilliance shine? What are they looking for in the culture of your company or in their own business? It is important, first and foremost, that you set up an environment that encourages honest, open dialogue. An environment where people can feel safe expressing their perspectives without fear of negative repercussions.

You should be explicit about and model your company's values. Incoming employees and partners can determine up front if those values resonate with them. This is not a one-time event. Even noble corporate goals such as "open communication, empathy, respect, innovation, or fostering an environment in which each individual is encouraged and supported to fulfill their potential" are open to interpretation, especially when being implemented.

Take the value of innovation, for example. How much risk tolerance do you and your company truly have? Being innovative often means straying far from proven methods and taking bold steps. There will be a lot of trial and error. Do you have the budget and mindset to accommodate that? If not, do not tout innovation as one of your key values.

Here are specific strategies I have employed in Corporate America and while running my own businesses to help create an environment for greatness.

1. We all know that not everyone learns and produces in the same way. However, I believe that everyone has the ability to do well when they are motivated and effectively supported. When I interview people to work with me, I begin by asking them what they need, what motivates them, and what they expect from me. I typically set this up as an exercise. For example, I may ask them, "What three things can I expect from you, and what three things do you expect from me?" It is great, time-efficient way for each person to give and receive concrete information while eliminating guesswork and assumptions.

2. I want everyone I hire to understand his or her importance to me and to the business, and I continually reinforce that. That does not mean that I do their work for them or otherwise cover up their mistakes. It means each one of us knows what is necessary to be productive and profitable, and we do our parts to make that happen. I have their backs and they have mine.

3. To benefit my coworkers and myself, I supply a steady stream of inspirational messages in the form of quotes,

images, or articles. Social media streamlines the process. Tag someone if you want to make sure they see your message. It may help them feel important and necessary.

4. I am generous with feedback. In the business world, and especially as an entrepreneur, it can be a lonely existence if no one tells you how awesome you are, at least once in a while. While constructive criticism is important, I find that positive feedback is out of this world. If your business has a newsletter, highlight something noteworthy that someone did. Give an award for something special, and thank people publicly for a job well done. A little praise can go a long way.

5. I nip problems in the bud—and privately. Business is filled with challenges. Before a challenge or issue gets out of hand, have a private conversation with the person or people at the root of or party to the matter, and iron out the wrinkles. The last thing you need is for something small to become monumental. I tell my new hires that I have an open door policy, and I encourage them to ask for my help with anything they feel they cannot handle themselves. When problems are left to fester, greatness will not happen.

6. I make discipline about accountability and growth rather than about punishment. While consequences may be needed for less than stellar output, there are ways to hold people accountable while also providing support. To offer an example from the insurance world, where minimal quotas must be met to ensure job security, fear can flare in agents' minds each time they do not close a deal. When I ran an insurance agency, I adopted a different approach and rewarded agents for writing business in ways that motivated them to see more people and thus enhanced their opportunities

to reach their quotas. My agents also were supported with weekly coaching sessions to troubleshoot challenges, establish accountability, and guide them to more sales. Inherent in every business are opportunities to hold others accountable while also encouraging success.

Each one of us is born with the potential for greatness. There are no exceptions. Yet most people realize less than ten percent of their potential, while a small handful of others rise to extraordinary heights. Why is that? Great leaders and business achievers look for something other than sales success as their ultimate goal. Their vision is to make a difference in the world, and they keep pushing forward to make it happen.

This is a good time to revisit and delve further into some of the questions first raised in the section about passion:

* What is your compelling "why" as a leader and in your business?

* What causes and issues are you willing to fight for?

* In what ways is your business a vehicle to make the world a better place?

* What are your core values as an individual and as a leader?

* What are the core values of your business or company?

* Are there any business goals or actions that are out of integrity with your core values? If so, how might you remedy that?

* How can your core values differentiate your business in the marketplace and attract like-minded employees, partners, and customers?

Achieving greatness requires self-awareness, discipline, and the support of others. Surround yourself with people who see your vision, believe in it, and will help you get there. As a leader, create environments where you enable others to thrive.

Leadership is about making others better as a result of your presence and making sure that impact lasts in your absence.
—Harvard Business School's Youngme Moon and Frances Frei

TWENTY-TWO

THE ART OF LISTENING

While most people say they listen effectively, many of us hear without truly listening. As Stephen Covey aptly writes, "Most people do not listen with the intent to understand; they listen with the intent to reply. They're either speaking or preparing to speak." This makes us hard of listening rather than hard of hearing. The rapid pace of business and increasingly brief modes of communication such as texts and tweets further complicate matters.

There is an art to listening well. It involves presence and attention. Leaders must listen well to lead well.

If you want to hone your listening skills, here are some ways to listen actively and communicate effectively.

1. Prepare yourself to listen. Relax, take a deep breath, or do whatever works for you to clear your mind so you can truly focus on the person speaking to you. Make sure you really are listening and not doing something else. It can be easy to multi-task, but the truth of the matter is you must concentrate on the other person to listen well.

2. Put the speaker at ease. Encourage the person speaking to do so freely. Remember they are trying to convey their needs, concerns, and feedback. Nod or use other gestures

or words to encourage them to continue. Maintain eye contact to show you are listening and understanding what is being said.

3. Don't talk; listen. You have two ears and one mouth for a reason. When somebody else is talking, do not interrupt, talk over them, or finish their sentences for them. Listen fully. When the other person has finished talking, ask questions or seek clarification if necessary to confirm you received their messages accurately.

4. Empathize. Try to understand the other person's point of view. Especially when it differs from yours. Look at issues from their perspective. Let go of preconceived ideas. When you have an open mind, you are more able to connect with the speaker. While you do not have to agree with everything being said, you should genuinely try to understand where they are coming from. If you were in their position, what might you need and want?

5. Be patient. A pause, even a long pause, does not necessarily mean that the speaker has finished. Be patient and let the speaker continue in his or her own time. They might be trying to figure out how to put their challenge into words. Never interrupt or finish a sentence for someone.

6. Listen for ideas, not just words. Your goal is to get the whole picture, not just a few bits and pieces. As an active listener, it is your job to link together pieces of information to reveal the ideas and intentions of others.

7. Watch for nonverbal communication. Studies show that fifty to sixty-five percent of communication is nonverbal.

Gestures, facial expressions, body language, and eye movements are all part of the message.

8. Ask open-ended questions. Follow up by asking questions that can deepen and advance the conversation.

9. Do not reply immediately. Instead of coming up with a "solution" right away, take a moment or two (or more if needed) to digest what you heard and more deeply consider the other person's perspectives. Think before you speak.

The suggestions above apply to everyone. We—and all our relationships, professionally and personally—benefit when we skillfully apply the art of listening in all our interactions. Yet as a gender communications expert, I would like to provide additional perspectives on differences in the ways men and women tend to communicate.

Consider the playground, where many boys and girls begin learning how to socialize. Young girls typically play in pairs or small groups, and they talk to connect. They play house and build relationships with other "moms" and their "babies" or dolls. Little boys tend to establish rapport with one another differently. Often they connect through physical activities, sports, and games. Is either way better or worse, right or wrong? Absolutely not. It's just different.

Now these girls and boys become women and men who must mesh their varying communication styles to work well together in the workplace. While many women tend to talk in narrative form, others are more get-to-the-bottom-line thinkers and listeners. While not all women are storytellers and not all men effectively cut to the chase, many studies have shown that more men are transactional and more women are relational in the way they communicate and conduct business. As a leader, it is important to cultivate an environment of mutual respect and understanding around varying communication styles.

Listening is a skill that men and woman alike must nurture on a continual basis to succeed in business and life. Listening well is fundamental to building healthy relationships and leading effectively. It is well worth the time and effort. Not getting it right can be disastrous. But when we get it right, we can get it right big time.

The most basic and powerful way to connect to another person is to listen. Just listen. Perhaps the most important thing we ever give each other is our attention.
—Rachel Naomi Remen

TWENTY-THREE

ASK QUESTIONS WITH PURPOSE

Early in my career I was given a nickname I cherish ... Question Queen. You see, I quickly realized that only by asking questions of my coworkers and customers could I learn what was needed and contribute meaningfully to the conversation. I asked every question I could think of to educate myself, help provide solutions, and be a valuable resource.

Asking someone thoughtful questions—then practicing the art of listening—demonstrates you care about them and what they have say. I am married to a retired United States Air Force Colonel, whom I affectionately refer to as the Colonel. How many people do you think ask the Colonel questions? Not many. Because when a Colonel "suggests" you do something, most people just do it. When we got married, his daughters would giggle and say, "Why do you ask him so many questions?" My response was, is, and will always be, "Because I am interested. When I stop asking questions, that's when you should begin to worry."

Asking questions when you know the answer (or think you do) can be a way to give others the opportunity to think about something they may otherwise not have. Many great leaders ask questions for this reason. In so doing, they invite other team members to step up, think strategically, and help solve problems. The best leaders listen carefully to their teams' responses and gain new perspectives and insights.

Given the value of asking questions, why don't more people ask questions? The reasons vary. Some people think it is a waste of time. They assume they know all they need to know, and they do not bother to ask more. I tell my clients all the time, "If you are the smartest person in the room, you are in the wrong room." Ask people questions and learn from them.

Others, especially women, are afraid that by asking questions they will appear weak, ignorant, or unsure. They fear that asking questions might introduce uncertainty or show them in a poor light.

Providing a different perspective, I have heard some people say that the reason some women ask a lot of questions is because those women are not confident about taking on the project or promotion, for example, until they receive reassurance from others.

Typically, both of the above are far from true. Asking questions is a sign of strength and intelligence, not a sign of weakness or uncertainty. Great leaders constantly ask questions and are well aware they do not have all the answers.

In an unhealthy workplace culture where employee morale is low, people may not ask questions because they are demotivated. They are not encouraged to succeed and do not have evidence that their supervisors value their opinions.

Finally, some people are in such a hurry to get things done that they do not stop to ask questions for fear it will slow them down. That is shortsighted. When I was being trained in sales years ago, I was taught, "Get in, get out, and get the check." That may have been fine if you didn't care about long-term relationships or client retention, but that is not the way of today's world.

Asking questions and continually learning and adapting are essential. However, many people do not know how to ask questions that yield valuable responses. May I offer some suggestions?

1. Do not ask multiple-choice questions. End your sentence at the question mark. It is okay, in fact often more effective, to be brief.

2. Get comfortable with silence. When you ask a question, give the person time to think, process, and respond. Do not jump in with another question or proposed solution until you really listen to their response to your initial question.

3. Start with "who, what, when, where, how, or why" for more in-depth answers. Questions that begin with these words help pave the way for more focused, detailed replies. Of course, if you simply want a yes or no reply, ask a question that will produce that.

4. If the response you receive still does not give you enough or the right kind of information, approach your inquiry from a different angle. Getting an incomplete answer gives you the opportunity to reframe your question or situation and approach it differently.

5. Make sure your questions are clear and easy to understand. Before you ask a question, know why you are asking it.

6. Direct your questions to a particular person. When questions are asked of an entire group, people may be reluctant to be the first to speak up.

7. Unless you have a good reason, questions should not be overly confrontational. These kinds of questions can cause significant communication problems.

8. Do not be afraid to ask a dumb question. The only truly dumb question is the important one that went unasked. Have you ever left a meeting and thought, "I should have asked … or why didn't I ask this?" I have. I then followed up with the people involved to continue the conversation and ensure everyone was equally informed.

Quality questions create a quality life. Successful people ask better questions, and as a result, they get better answers.
—Anthony Robbins

TWENTY-FOUR

THE POWER OF STORYTELLING IN BUSINESS

As a speaker, author, and businesswoman, I know how important it is to connect with your audience. And by audience, I am referring as much to a large room of people as I am to the one person you may be meeting with, i.e., the audience of one. In terms of your tools for connecting, I am referring to the words and images you employ, both spoken and written, as well as to the underlying meanings, emotions, and messages.

I listen to other speakers and read a lot of books. Some get it and some don't. Want to know the difference? The ones who get it tell a story that creates an experience and powerfully, memorably conveys their message.

What is the secret to telling a great story? Make the story come alive. Give it personality. While people may forget facts, they will not forget a great story.

What are some of the building blocks to crafting stories you want to share?

1. The Why. What is the purpose of the story? Share that purpose with the audience. You can be as obvious as saying,

"Here is an example of ..." or "I would like to tell you story to illustrate ..."

2. The What. What actually happened? The worst thing you can do is tell a story that isn't really a story. By that I mean you get lost in details or tangents, stray too far from your point, and lose your audience along the way.

3. The How. Have a clear beginning, middle, and end to your tale. In the beginning, set the stage by introducing the situation or problem. The middle is where you bring the problem or scenario to life. Describe what happened and how it made you feel. Be sure that the problem you are discussing is relevant and relatable to your audience. The ending should be as brief as the beginning. Describe the resolution and connect it back to your purpose for sharing it. This is where takeaways come into play.

4. The Who. Who are the characters in your story? What happened to them? What did they overcome? Try not to always be the hero of your stories. Let your audience know about some of your mistakes and failures. Those make great stories, especially when you reveal how you handled failure and turned things around.

5. The Where. Paint a picture. Describe the scene or setting in detail so the audience can see and feel what you are talking about. Your goal is to evoke a palpable, lasting connection.

Above all, your stories and all your communication should be relevant and true. The more you tap into your sincere desire to connect with and serve the person or people with whom you are speaking, the more meaningful and memorable your communication and connection will be.

Some of the greatest lessons in our lives come from stories we have been told. Especially those that affect us emotionally or inspire us. While we may not remember all the specific details of these stories, we do tend to remember their purpose and key takeaways. We personally benefit as we incorporate those teachings into our lives, and we pay it forward as we share the wisdom with others.

We cannot create a world we can't imagine,
and stories are the engines of our imaginations.
—Josh Stearns

TWENTY-FIVE

FOLLOWERSHIP

Followership is the other side of leadership. It is the ability to take direction well, be part of a team, and deliver what is expected of you. Here is something to ponder, "How well the followers follow is just as important for success as how well the leaders lead."

It is easy to enjoy praise for great leadership. But how would you feel if someone said you were an excellent follower? Can you be both a great leader and a great follower? Absolutely, depending on the situation. Can you be both a weak leader and a weak follower? This answer to this is also yes, depending on the situation.

What are some qualities of a good follower? Expect to see similarities between a good follower and a good leader.

1. The ability to take direction while also exercising good judgment. There is a difference between following the leader even if you don't fully agree with their approach versus blindly following if you are asked to do something illegal or unethical.

2. A strong work ethic. You likely will find it difficult to be a good follower if you are not a strong worker.

3. Discretion. Knowing when not to speak can be as important as knowing when to speak. Certain situations may arise wherein keeping things confidential is important.

4. Loyalty. Good followers respect their obligations and have a strong allegiance to their leader and their team.

5. Ego in check. Good followers keep their egos in check. They are team players and realize it is not all about them.

I gravitate toward leadership roles. Leading is part of my personality and my training, and I flourish in this capacity. However, I recently was given a wonderful opportunity to practice followership at a conference I attend annually. In prior years I have been the keynote speaker, facilitated breakout sessions, and been a vendor. This year, though, I was asked to play the supporting role of follower.

I realized this role was critical because if I could demonstrate my ability to take direction, be loyal to the cause, and keep my ego in check, I would contribute to a positive outcome for all. The new leader would feel supported and confident in her role, and others would follow. I am happy to report the conference turned out beautifully.

While some may think followership lies in the shadow of leadership, it is equally important. There are no leaders without followers. We all know that businesses are only as good as their leadership, but leadership depends on great followership as well.

When I worked in the corporate world of insurance, I was both a leader and a follower. I led my fellow agents by providing sales training and coaching. I also reported to a leader who was in charge of all training.

Having worked my way up from sales, I had tremendous credibility. Each day I did my best to model integrity and character as I helped the agents grow. I knew my strengths, and I engaged others to assist in areas where I was weaker. I had the experience the agents hungered for. I had not only been there and done that, I bought the T-shirt as well, and I shared what I learned with them.

Great leaders tend to attract great followers. I am most inclined to be led by someone with character, who acknowledges their strengths and makes accommodations for their weaknesses, who is committed to my growth, and who has the experience, skills, and vision to guide me.

People do not just follow anyone. As a leader, you must give them a good reason to follow you. Many times people are placed into leadership roles and expect their teams will follow them simply because they have the title. It does not work that way—at least not with deep, lasting success.

Leadership is as much about being the person that people want to follow, as it is about knowing where the team is headed.

I must follow the people. Am I not their leader?
—British Prime Minister Benjamin Disraeli

PART 5

DECISIVENESS

Should I quit my job or stay where I am? Should I have cereal for dinner, or is it really only for breakfast? Should I put my bonus check in the bank or reward myself for a job well done? We are regularly faced with choices. For the more significant decisions, we may carefully consider the possibilities. Yet some decisions seem so easy we wonder if there could be a catch, so we analyze those as well. We probably all have experienced times of complete mental overwhelm, when it feels as if we cannot possibly make one more decision in that moment.

When my daughter still lived at home and would ask me on occasion where I wanted to meet her for dinner, I would automatically say, "It doesn't matter. Whatever restaurant you want to go to is fine with me." There were some problems with that reply.

First, I am a vegetarian so it actually did matter. Second, not any place is fine with me because I do not enjoy over-the-top restaurants or ones with a two-hour wait. Most troublesome, I was conveying that my opinion didn't matter to me when, in fact, it did.

I rationalized that it wasn't worth risking having an argument about dinner. After all, I love my daughter so much, don't see her that often, and was taught to pick my battles. Of course, not making a decision is also a choice. Occasionally my choice to avoid choosing led to the disagreement I was trying to avoid.

I began considering other situations where I took a back seat by not expressing my preference or making a decision. Just because the matter at hand wasn't earth shattering, did that mean I shouldn't express myself? How might others view my indecisiveness?

I know I am not alone in my now former habit of disregarding my interests and avoiding making a decision. Many women do this throughout their personal and professional lives. Sure, it can be satisfying to collaborate, solicit opinions, and receive support from others, but as a leader you have to take a stand and make decisions even when it is uncomfortable.

Being decisive does not mean you are a control freak or that everything must go your way or the highway. It simply means you make a decision. You may not end up loving all your decisions. Mistakes or missteps are inevitable, but the people who work with and for you likely will appreciate a leader who creates opportunities by being decisive.

While great decisions can lead to terrific results, decisions that are less than great can create opportunities for valuable lessons learned. Some people refer to this as course correcting. As I previously mentioned, when this happens to me, I like to have a little fun with it by declaring, "Plot twist!"

If you are procrastinating on making an important decision at work, what if you put a time limit on it? You don't have to share your decision-making timeline with everyone, but if you do (providing the subject matter is appropriate to share with others), you just might see more teamwork emerge to get related tasks completed and on time.

I recently came across a *New York Times* article in which Therese Huston reviews studies that answer the question, "Are Women Better Decision Makers?" The studies show that, under stress, there are gender differences and women tend to perform better. In stressful situations, women typically take smaller, measured risks and are more able to consider another person's perspective. Men tend to take bigger risks for bigger wins, even when they are more costly and unlikely. She concludes with a study that revealed large-cap companies with at least one woman on their boards significantly outperformed comparable companies with all-male boards.

There you have it.

*It's better to be boldly decisive and risk being wrong
than to agonize at length and be right too late.*
—Marilyn Moats Kennedy

TWENTY-SIX
THE POWER OF CHOICES

The average working adult makes roughly twelve decisions first thing each morning and at least seventy decisions throughout the day. While these statistics vary considerably depending on each person and their respective responsibilities, we all face numerous decisions daily.

The first decision may be seemingly as simple as, "Do I get out of bed now or hit the snooze button on my alarm?" From the moment we wake, we start deciding how we want our day to unfold.

There is an old saying, "If the first thing you do each morning is eat a live frog, you can go through the day with the satisfaction of knowing that is probably the worst thing that will happen to you all day!" Your "frog" is the one thing you are most likely to procrastinate on if you do not take immediate action. It also may be the one task that can have the greatest positive impact in that moment.

It also has been said, "If you have to eat two frogs, eat the ugliest one first!" This is another way of saying that if you have two important tasks before you, start with the biggest, hardest, and most important task. Discipline yourself to begin promptly and complete the task before moving on to something else.

While this can be useful, yet hard-to-swallow advice (pun intended) regarding how to decide which task to do first, decision-making entails much more than what to do in what order. When I first started working in a corporate environment, I treated the company as if it were my own. I felt a strong sense of responsibility regarding my role and my team's contributions to the company's bottom line.

I created various metrics and checklists, and my white board was never empty. My to-do list was ever expanding. I was eating bigger and uglier frogs, and the faster I crossed things off my lists, the faster new tadpoles were jumping aboard.

In that frenzied state, I started to feel inauthentic and increasingly uncomfortable with what I was saying and doing. While my intentions were pure, my execution was flawed. I needed to make some changes. Even though I was receiving terrific reviews from my team and the thousands of people I was training, I knew I could do better ... not more ... but better.

So I sat myself down and went back to the beginning. What was I supposed to be doing, and how would I make a difference and bring value? I looked at my to-do lists and checklists and noticed I had added tasks that didn't belong to me. Although they were tasks I knew how to do, they were taking my time and experience away from what I did best. Why would I continue to do that? The only result I could see if I were to continue with the status quo was that I would not bring my full value. I had promised myself that when I stopped bringing real value, I would stop doing what I was doing.

That was a pivotal moment in my career. I locked myself in my office to revamp everything I was doing. I took the things that did not belong on my lists and delegated them to their rightful owners (complete with the checklists of course). That alone gave me back five to eight hours a week to redirect to what I most needed to do—create training programs, coach agents, and deliver trainings in person and virtually. I was back on track, feeling so much better and absolutely authentic.

My daily to-do list no longer looked like a census sheet. Instead, it had precisely my priorities. I returned to eating one or two frogs each day. Life tasted so much better.

How might you revamp your daily decision-making regimen?

First, listen to your gut. Many of us refer to this as our sixth sense. When you are meeting someone or trying to make a serious decision, your gut can be a valuable barometer ... if you listen to it. Unfortunately, I learned the hard way that choosing to disregard or go against my gut wreaks havoc, or at a minimum, causes considerable stress.

Once when I was offered a contract to provide trainings for a company, I was initially super excited about it and too hastily agreed to do it. After I sat down and more fully considered the opportunity (that I had already said yes to), I had to admit it had nothing to do with my Selling In A Skirt brand or my material.

Even though the terms of the contract were great on paper, my gut was yelling at me to step away from the assignment.

At first I tried to ignore my gut and rationalize I could make the assignment work. But I couldn't overlook the back pains, stomachaches, and the feeling I can only describe as an alien screaming inside me. When I decided to go back to the company and respectfully explain why I needed to decline the contract, my gut was happy again and so was I.

In conjunction with listening to your gut, gather all the facts. To make an informed decision, learn as much as you can. I am not talking about running a background check on a potential date. Rather, I am referring to big decisions like changing careers or investigating medical treatment options. Being informed is being responsible.

Next, use the trusty method of writing down a list of pros and cons. Not only can this help clarify factors in the decision you are facing, it may also uncover additional possibilities.

After I make my lists (which can be a very linear process), I check back in with my gut. Then I take full responsibility for my decision.

I encourage you to do the same. Especially as a leader, it is imperative that you take responsibility for your decisions. While you may want to talk things over with trusted colleagues or friends during your decision-making process, remember that ultimately the choice you make is your own. Make sure you are making the best decision you can with the information you have and not taking an easy way out to avoid leaving your comfort zone.

Finally, give yourself permission to make mistakes. No one is perfect. Attempting to be is impossible and exhausting. If you make a mistake, make a change. I always say that every mistake I have made has been a lesson learned. I bet you will not make the same mistake twice, and if you do, perhaps there was another lesson embedded in it. My 3Rs are review, readjust, and release.

I also have found the 5 Whys to be useful. It is an iterative, problem-solving technique developed by Sakichi Toyoda and used by Toyota Motor Corporation during the evolution of its manufacturing methodologies. Other companies also use the technique in varying forms.

Why practice the 5 Whys? For starters, it is simple and anyone can do it. It is known as practical problem solving. With each step, you uncover the next level of the issue and start to see the root cause.

The process is to ask why, then continue with four more whys, going deeper into the matter at hand. You can pose the questions to yourself or serve as a sounding board for someone else. If that's the case, you allow the other person to answer your first why before you ask another. You both may be surprised by what is uncovered.

Here is an example of how I used this exercise when I was given a promotion.

1. Why do I want this promotion? So I can have a bigger impact on my team.

2. Why? My veteran team members will be well supported in growing their books of business and becoming more successful. My new team members will receive proper training right from the start.

3. Why? I can use my experiences to benefit others, and I can share the advantages of being a successful woman in sales.

4. Why? My goal is always to bring value to my team at all levels.

5. Why? Bringing value to others is important to me. It is one of my core values.

You are where you are today because of the choices you have made. One of the wonderful things about life is that since it presents us with so many decisions daily, we regularly have opportunities to choose differently. You can look for a new job, start eating more healthfully, or take a different route home.

But many times we do not make a different choice and instead just complain because the choice to complain is the path of least resistance. Too many people choose to live their lives "as-is" when "as-is" is not ideal because they fear the unknown. Some may fear failing. When we allow our fears to control us, we are choosing to live a life that is not all it could be. Don't fall victim to fear or defeatism.

This reminds me of a story I once heard about twin brothers. One was extremely successful and wealthy. When asked what motivated his success, he replied, "My father was an alcoholic. I had no choice." In contrast, his twin brother could not hold down a job and became an alcoholic. When asked, "What caused you to become an alcoholic?" he replied, "My father was an alcoholic. I had no choice." There is a great message here. What do you really want? What choices are you making to realize your desires?

Do your best to make healthy, wise, responsible decisions. It is not always easy, but you always have the choice.

I am who I am today because of the choices I made yesterday.
—Eleanor Roosevelt

TWENTY-SEVEN
CHOOSING FREEDOM

Before we get into more strategies for decision-making, I want to discuss freedom. Freedom means different things to different people. It is important to know what it means for you.

There is no singular, definitive list of the types of freedoms people want to experience. Personal, societal, and cultural circumstances all play a role. Yet here is a list of some of the aspects of freedom people frequently cite as desirable.

1. Financial. This one often tops the list. You choose whether or not to take the steps to attain it.

2. Relational. It is human nature to want to experience loving relationships, whether with a spouse, child, friends, and/or through your career.

3. Temporal. Even though we all have twenty-four hours in a day, some people accomplish a lot while others complain they do not have enough time.

4. Geographic. Many of us feel like we are stuck where we live because we were born there or have lived there for many years. We are afraid to venture beyond our bubble even when we know it is not the best place for us.

5. Health. We all want to be healthy and active. Some people take the necessary steps to accomplish that, while others do not. Some of us are born with health challenges and do everything in our power to be as healthy as possible, while others do not.

6. Freedom from oppression. Being able to live a life that is true to ourselves, our families, and our traditions is something we all cherish. People who differ from the norm often are judged, feared, or mistreated. Those who judge often are inaccurate in their assessment. If you can learn from someone else, be open to it. We are more alike than we are different.

These are just some of the freedoms many of us seek. Some people are fortunate to experience a few of these, while others have them all. It comes down to the choices we make for ourselves.

What should you do if you find yourself in a situation that feels constricting or limiting? If you long for freedom and know you need to make changes, but you aren't sure how to begin?

Here are some suggestions:

* Recognize and control your fear. Initiating or even contemplating change can trigger fear. Whether you are planning to start a new career, move to a new city, or embark on a new relationship, you will be taking a risk. It is normal to feel some anxiety, but do not let it sidetrack you. Baby steps are fine.

* Remember where you came from. Reflect on your past and consider both what's working and what's not in your current situation. Learn from your experiences, and retain or replicate the positives as you move forward.

* Erase negativity. Concentrate on staying as positive as possible. Banish negative voices from your mind. It is time to build your confidence. Consider how even the word "impossible" includes the message, "I'm possible."

* Think about the things in your life for which you are grateful. Even the seemingly smallest things. Write them down each day. Positive attracts positive.

* Take a close look at the relationships around you. Who in your life is a source of support, and who is an energy vampire? When you want to release habits or patterns that no longer serve you, it is especially important to surround yourself with people who can help you define and work toward your new goals.

* Do not delay. No one knows how long we have on this earth. Do not wait until the time is perfect, the planets are aligned, and you are at your all-time best. Take action each day toward the new, freer future you envision.

Even with the best intentions and planning, missteps are inevitable. They are part of the process. If you make a mistake once, it is simply a mistake. If you continue to do so repeatedly, it becomes a choice you are making.

Think about it this way. Nobody can go back and start a new beginning, but anyone can start today and make a new ending.

I do have the freedom to choose
what I want to do, and I'll continue to do that.
—Moira Kelly

TWENTY-EIGHT

STRATEGIC PLANNING

I don't know about you, but I am not a strategist. I am an implementer who prefers to implement rather than strategize any day. Yet strategic planning is essential for business success.

I am married to the greatest strategic thinker there is, but when he wants to "chat" about my business I cringe. I know we need to, I know it is important, but still I find it uncomfortable and challenging.

A good strategic plan projects at least two to five years out and describes in detail how your business will grow and prosper. It should cover where you want to go and why, how you plan to get there, projected costs and income, anticipated challenges, and how you intend to address them.

While your plan should be written out with sufficient specificity, it need not be a leather-bound, two-hundred-page document. As long as it is carefully considered and has clear action steps, it can be as brief as a few pages. Alternately, it can be in the form of a deck of PowerPoint slides if that works better for you.

Here are ten easy steps to developing a strategic plan.

1. Identify what your business can potentially do better than any other company. What makes you the best? You must understand why customers come to you rather than your competitors.

2. Write your mission statement. What do you plan to offer your clients?

To write a mission statement, you should answer these questions:

* What is your business?
* What are you trying to accomplish for your customers?
* What is your reason for existing as a company?
* What are your business goals beyond income generation?

3. Write your vision statement. This is your long-range vision for your business, including your areas of focus and the market space you want to occupy. To write a vision statement, you should answer the following question: What will our business look like in two to five years?

4. It is time for SWOT. Look carefully at your company's strengths, weaknesses, opportunities, and threats. Think about what you do best and where there are opportunities to do that even better.

5. What solutions do your customers seek? What can you give them that your competition cannot? Think about who your customers are and describe them in detail. What

would make your business stand out for them with respect to the solutions they desire? I am a big advocate of asking rather than guessing. Ask your customers questions, and carefully listen to their answers. If your product or service is not exactly what they need, tweak it.

6. Write down your top three goals and corresponding objectives. Writing them down can begin to shift them from fantasy to reality. I suggest you keep it to three goals and three objectives for each goal to optimize your chances for success. With each goal, come up with just three objectives or action steps needed to reach the goal. Your listed items should be SMART, which stands for specific, measurable, achievable, results-oriented, and time-conscious.

7. Identify your resources. Do you have sufficient resources to follow through with your stated goals and objectives? This is where your relationships come in. If you don't personally have the resources or knowledge you need, it's important to know where or to whom you can turn. Will they respond to you if you reach out? It is so much easier and more enjoyable to build relationships before you need them.

8. Take action. This is music to the ears for all you implementers out there. It certainly is for me. This is where we take our to-do lists of goals and objectives and get cracking. Which items have your name on them? Which ones are you going to outsource and to whom? It is wise to write down the action plan and share it with your team members and other contributing parties.

9. Periodically review your goals. To ensure your goals are not just measurable, but also measured, review them

on a regular basis. If you are ahead of the game, keep going. If you are behind the eight ball, you may need to call in some assistance.

10. Remember, strategy is your friend. Do not put it up on a shelf until someone reminds you to find it. Develop a positive relationship with strategic planning and find the support you need to integrate it into your business life. If you do not yet have a personal board of directors to hold you accountable, it may be time to assemble one.

Now that we have covered the basics of creating a solid, actionable, not-too-complicated strategic plan, I want to introduce you to the Strategic Triangle. Be careful how you use it because it has caused more than one person, including myself, to rethink a new venture.

I have a tendency to be distracted by shiny objects—or to be more accurate, shiny business opportunities. As a business leader, and especially as an entrepreneur, staying focused is critical. My gut tends to tell me when I have gone astray. If I agree to do something that is not true to my niche, my body reacts. It's similar to heartburn but with an added attraction. The sensation feels like a lot of jumping around inside that moves toward my back. I have been reduced to tears by how uncomfortable this makes me. Whenever this occurs, I recognize it as a clear signal I am not focused on my primary target.

To help ensure I stay on track, my business coach led me through a strategy session in which we defined what I am "allowed" to do in my business. It is called my Strategic Triangle.

A triangle has three angles, and the rule is that anything I do in my business has to fit into one of those angles. My triangle is speaking, coaching, and training. If an opportunity comes along that does not fit into one of those categories, I cannot do it. If I want to add something to my triangle, I have to eliminate something else. My Strategic Triangle has helped me keep business priorities and opportunities at the forefront, so I can get the important things done.

We have a strategic plan. It's called "doing things."
—Herb Kelleher

TWENTY-NINE

ACCOUNTABILITY PARTNERS
AND MASTERMIND GROUPS

A section on decisiveness would be incomplete if it did not address accountability. Decision-making and accountability go hand in hand, especially in the context of leadership. Not only are strong leaders decisive, but they also take responsibility for their decisions. They hold themselves accountable for the decisions they make—regardless of the outcomes—and they hold themselves accountable to their employees, colleagues, customers, and shareholders.

I personally have found that accountability partners and mastermind groups have been invaluable to me. Perhaps you are wondering, "What exactly is a mastermind group?" Typically, it is a tight-knit, supportive group of individuals committed to doing and being their best. They also are committed to assisting their fellow group member achieve their goals. Mastermind groups offer a combination of brainstorming, peer accountability, and support. Participants challenge each other to set and accomplish ambitious goals.

While each one of us is ultimately responsible for our own success and growth, having someone (or several people) hold us accountable can provide an extra push in the right direction. In fact, being accountable to others can lead to success on steroids! According to a study by Dominican University of California, seventy-six percent of those who mapped out their goals in writing and sent a weekly progress report to a friend accomplished their goals or were at least halfway there within four weeks. In contrast, only thirty-five percent of the study participants who kept their goals to themselves without writing them down could claim the same success.

Some people thrive when they work with a group or accountability posse, while others prefer one-on-one attention from an accountability buddy or partner. If the latter applies to you, here are suggestions for finding a good match in an accountability partner.

1. Try to find someone outside your field since they may be more objective and better able to provide fresh perspectives on your business.

2. Find someone who will be brutally honest with you. While you want someone to tell you when you are doing a good job, it may be more important for them to tell you when you are off-kilter, perhaps saying something like, "Are you kidding?"

3. Be very clear about expectations from the beginning. For example, what are each of you willing to do, what are the deal breakers, when should you each be in listening mode versus offering feedback, and when and how will you meet and check in with each other?

4. Establish mutually-agreed-upon consequences. Think of things that will motivate you to never fall short of your stated commitments. They can be silly consequences, like wearing a tutu to a football game or dyeing your hair ... trust me, those would be motivators.

My accountability partners have helped me grow my business through their guidance and expertise, and they hold me to my commitments. I, in turn, do the same for them. Accountability partners can be your secret weapons for faster growth. Once you decide to do something and say it out loud, your buddies are going to pick up on the promise you made and hold you to it.

When I was writing my second book, I casually mentioned to my mastermind group that I wanted to complete it by February first. Well they did not see this as casual. They heard my target date loud and clear and asked specific questions about my timeline, my marketing plan, and so on. I realized right then and there that my book *would* be completed by February first. It is not even, "Ask and you shall receive." It is more like, "Tell and you will have the support to get it done."

This may sound like an ideal environment in which to grow your business and yourself. It can be. Yet you must be open to receiving suggestions and ideas, and you need to actively offer your opinions, insights, and experience to the members of the group. Of course, it is also important that the mastermind group you want to get involved with is one that will benefit you.

You will want a group whose members have a wide range of expertise. Some of the members may even be people you might never otherwise cross paths with. That can be a great thing. However, if you think you will feel intimidated by the other members, you probably will not get the experience you are looking for.

Now here is the fun part. As a member, you contribute your experience, expertise, and value to the other members. Guess who benefits from this? Everyone. Including you. You may find this similar to mentoring in that sometimes you learn more from your mentees than they learn from you.

In a mastermind group, the challenges someone else faces may not even be on your radar now, but you will have insight when and if they do surface in your life. Perhaps more importantly, even without an issue brewing in your business, you often will learn things in conversation that can enhance what you already are doing.

Something we discuss on a regular basis in my mastermind group is fear. Regardless of its source, fear is much more difficult to navigate when facing it alone. A mastermind group can provide valuable insight and perspective. Since the other group members are not as close to or attached to your business, they see things through far more objective eyes. And as I mentioned earlier, one of the biggest benefits of a mastermind group is accountability. For some people, that is the primary reason to join one.

So how does a mastermind group actually work? Groups typically meet on a regular basis. While meeting in person is optimal, technology allows for groups to connect via Skype or other online mediums. Some groups meet monthly or quarterly, while others meet weekly or biweekly. It depends on the group's expectations and desired outcomes.

Having participated in several mastermind groups over the years, I have found I prefer to meet at least once a month, and that diversity among the members is important. While

I love connecting with others in my business or industry, it is not necessarily the best recipe for a mastermind group.

Being part of a mastermind group is priceless because the members can save you time, money, and pulling your hair out. The value lies both in the members and the dynamics of the group. The general goal tends to be on long-term success and relationships, not quick fixes. Mastermind groups can provide you with reassurance that you are making sound decisions and covering all of your bases before making an important move.

What are some characteristics of a solid mastermind group? A key feature is that it is exclusive—but not in an elitist way. The group should not be open to everyone. Those who participate should be aligned in their overall goals and motivations. Not everyone is or should be part of a mastermind group. You likely would not want to include people who are negative, are not really present, or do not look forward to the meetings.

Here are some other characteristics of a solid mastermind group:

* Members are peers.

* Members have varying business backgrounds and skill sets.

* Members are able and willing to put in the time.

* Members have a mentor mindset.

* Members are as eager to provide advice as to receive it.

* Members enjoy solving problems.

* Members are good collaborators.

* Members mutually respect and trust one another.

Mastermind groups can help you continually learn and grow both professionally and personally. By regularly participating and sharing your challenges, it is almost certain that someone in your mastermind group will have meaningful suggestions for you, just as you likely will be able to offer solutions, connections, or tactics to help others.

You also may discover you think bigger. You cannot help but stretch beyond your boundaries when you are surrounded by motivated people doing amazing things.

The next best thing to being wise oneself
is to live in a circle of those who are.
—C.S. Lewis

PART 6

RESILIENCE

According to *Merriam-Webster*, resilience means "an ability to recover from or adjust easily to misfortune or change." Are we ever truly prepared? There are those who say you should always have a Plan B, while others who say there are twenty-six other letters in the alphabet so not to worry if A or B do not work out. Still others claim that if you consider anything in addition to your original plan, you are setting yourself up for failure. Which camp are you in? I am a firm believer that no matter how well things are going for you right now—or how less than perfect they are—life happens, so don't get too comfy.

Unexpected stuff inevitably arises and affects each one of us, our jobs, and our families. When it does, it may be tempting to grab your favorite blanket and run back to bed. But the reality is, that is just avoiding reality. So we talk to our friends, coaches, spouses, or whoever can lend an ear. We hope they offer us wisdom or at least buoy us for the moment.

As a leader, the way you navigate setbacks sets an example for others. Resilient people look at difficulties as challenges. Rather than allowing challenges to define them, they approach hard times as opportunities to grow and learn.

Resilient people do not take their commitments to their personal or professional goals lightly. When setbacks happen, they try to turn them into comebacks. They are discerning and focus on the areas in which they have at least some control and can exert their influence.

In the pages that follow, I will guide you in how to manage and recover from setbacks—and even how to learn to fail. But before we go there, I will provide specific recommendations for you to exercise excellent self-care, prevent burnout, sidestep potentially avoidable setbacks, and be prepared to handle life's curve balls.

She stood in the storm, and when the wind did not blow her way, she adjusted her sails.
—Elizabeth Edwards

THIRTY

TAKE CARE OF YOURSELF SO YOU
CAN TAKE CARE OF BUSINESS

I would like to share a personal story about the exact moment I realized I needed to take better care of myself. For some people, a health scare provides a wake-up call. For others, it may be a financial crisis or the dissolution of a marriage. In my case the messenger was far friendlier but equally effective.

It was 2009. My children were grown and out of the house. I could dedicate myself completely to creating and launching Selling In A Skirt. I was eager to pour my experience and passion into my business of helping women succeed in sales, with no one and nothing else vying for my attention. I was on fire, moving full steam ahead.

Then it happened. One of my best friends came for a visit. Alisa and I had been friends as well as professional colleagues for decades. Although we had been trying to coordinate a visit for some time, we could not seem to get our schedules to cooperate as I lived in Dallas and she in Tennessee. Finally, on this particular weekend, the sun, moon, and planets were aligned.

We were all set for a fun weekend of wine, food, and chocolate ... and more wine. We were going to solve all the problems of the world, or if we couldn't accomplish that, at least we would talk about relationships and business. Alisa has a wonderful marriage and was building a new business, and she wanted to brainstorm with me. I knew I could help with her budding business, and I was excited to share my latest business progress with her.

As I welcomed her to my new home and gave her the grand tour, she complimented me on nearly everything about it. After touring my closet and deciding which outfits we would share going forward, we settled into the living room, filled our wine glasses, and began talking about business. She told me how proud she was of all I had accomplished. I reciprocated. Then she said something utterly unexpected.

In her deep, deliberate Southern drawl, she said, "Girl ... you have everything ... but you have nothing."

Her words were like a knife to my stomach. Even though I knew she was not being malicious—she does not have a mean bone in her body—that one sentence cut to the chase of a void I had not even realized I had been filling with my incessant work. Somewhere along the way, I had lost sight of myself and any semblance of a personal life. Where did I fit into my vision of success? Where did I fit into my own life? Where was I period?

In that very moment, I knew I had to make significant changes. I needed to find time for myself, my children, a personal life, and the things I cared about outside of work. Yet while rediscovering these aspects of my life, I also wanted to continue to build and grow my business successfully.

The changes started with taking control of my calendar, and I was as strict as I could be. Did I ever fall off the wagon? Of course. I love my work, so it is to be expected. But ever since that fateful day in my living room, I always make a concerted effort to find time for what is important to me as a woman as well as a businesswoman.

Sometimes we need someone objective to point out the obvious. Without Alisa's savvy observation, I don't how my life would look now. What I do know is that Alisa's comment came at just the right time to jolt me out of a long pattern of overwork and remind me that life is fundamentally about creating memories and moments with the people you love by doing what you love and by loving yourself enough to say yes to you.

When I learned this lesson—and every situation, good or bad, has a lesson—I opened myself up for new opportunities. As I began to allow other people to enter my very private world, wonderful things started happening. Both my personal and professional lives began to change.

It was as if I was looking through a different lens. I could still work when and how I wanted, and I also had a reason to stop. I began dating again and fell in love with the man I would marry. He not only changed my personal outlook, but as I previously mentioned, he also helped me become more strategic in my business.

Of course, taking control of my calendar was just the first step. I also revisited my sleeping, eating, and exercise routines. I looked at my life holistically and concluded, "Everything I do is dependent on everything I do." Does that make sense? It did to me.

After I entered everything I did into my calendar, I could see where I was out of balance. This helped me create my own self-imposed boundaries with respect to when I wouldn't work and when I would. For example, after deciding to start each day with something that is one hundred percent for me, I now do not even look at my computer until I finish on my treadmill. That was just one of the things I needed to change.

If work is taking over your life and you want to rebalance, where might you begin?

Here are a few suggestions.

1. What are you eating? If you do not fuel your body properly, nothing else matters. I make sure to eat well, and while that may take a little more time out of my schedule, I know that it's worth it. When I feel good, I work better. Skipping meals takes me to Code Red. Not fun. When that occurs, not only do I suffer, but so does my business. Be careful about drinking too much alcohol because that leads to poor habits. You and your business will pay the price.

2. Are you sleeping enough? I was surviving on four to five hours of sleep a night. According to the National Institutes of Health, "After several nights of losing sleep, even a loss of just one to two hours per night, your ability to function suffers as if you haven't slept at all for a day or two." I figured I lost a few years at the rate I was going.

On one hand, I was thrilled by how much I thought I was accomplishing when I slept less, but I suffered by burning the candle at both ends. I may not be the life of the party these days since I am generally in bed by 9:30 p.m., but I do feel and work better.

One more sleep tip. Try going to bed and waking up at the same time each day. It helps get your body back into a healthy rhythm.

3. Do something just for you each morning. Many of my friends read or meditate in the morning. They begin each day uncovering their intention for the day or reflecting on what was, what is, and what could be. I love my morning routine on the treadmill. While I may not be fully concentrating on my innermost thoughts, at least I am away from my computer for forty-five minutes in the morning while also getting exercise.

4. If your "just for you" morning activity does not involve exercise, make sure to schedule regular exercise into your week. This is probably the most common carryover item on everyone's to-do lists. Find something you enjoy (perhaps walking, a dance class, weightlifting, or yoga) and maybe even an exercise buddy who can be your physical fitness accountability partner.

According to *Harvard Business Review*, studies show "our mental firepower is directly linked to our physical regimen. And nowhere are the implications more relevant than to our performance at work. Consider the following cognitive benefits, all of which you can expect as a result of incorporating regular exercise into your routine: improved concentration, sharper memory, faster learning, prolonged mental stamina, enhanced creativity, and lower stress. Exercise has also been shown to elevate mood, which has serious implications for workplace performance."

5. Are you involved in activities and building relationships outside of work? Do you have close friends? If you don't know where to meet people, here are a few ideas. Take a look at Cousin Google to discover networking opportunities in your area. You also can go to meetup.com to see who has formed a group on a topic of interest to you. If you don't find what you are seeking, you can start your own group on meetup.com. We live in a well-connected world. Open yourself up to new experiences.

6. Invest in learning something new. Take classes, go to a seminar, sign up for an online course, or create your own path to exploring your interests. You may be surprised where your new skills take you.

7. Finally, what is really important to you? Is there a cause you care deeply about? How might you be involved? Even when you make the time to eat right, sleep well, exercise, and make friends, you still might feel like something is missing.

I am passionate about women starting out in the work environment. Mentoring young women has been a tremendous pleasure and honor for me. At one point a few years ago, I was officially and unofficially mentoring four women simultaneously. You may be thinking that it was a lot of work, but showing them the ropes not only helped me remember some things I took for granted, it also led me back to some of the basics I forgot. It was a win-win situation all the way around. Since self-care was not modeled for me when I was beginning my career, I emphasized its value to my mentees.

Here are some of the benefits I shared with them about investing in oneself and practicing self-care:

* You are letting people know that the way you treat yourself is the way they should treat you. Respect is earned. Once others see that you respect yourself, you can earn theirs as well.

* You know what you need better than anyone else. Don't wait for anyone else's approval of how to care for you.

* You are demonstrating that you prioritize who and what is really important to you.

* You become a magnet, attracting the right people and opportunities into your life. You know what is right for you and what is not. You become unafraid to say no to your deal breakers. You do not compromise your values or integrity.

When you take care of yourself first, you will accomplish and enjoy more professionally and personally. By eliminating negativity in your life, you will have more time and energy to complete the projects that can help propel you and your business to the next level.

Taking care of yourself is the best selfish thing you can do.
—Author Unknown

THIRTY-ONE

PREVENT OR RECOVER
FROM BURNOUT

The other day I was with a client who was preparing to launch a new product. The content was great. The name? Not so much. She knew she had to bring more creativity to the naming process, but she was out of juice.

How can you be creative and get your message across when the last thing you feel is creative, and you are sure that being productive left on the last train out?

We all know what it feels like to be on our A game. For me, it might mean pumping out articles and creating new content, new programs, and new directions. Then suddenly it stops. You hit a wall. Maybe you pushed yourself too hard for too long. For the time being, your well has run dry. You know you must refill it but don't know where to begin.

By incorporating the self-care strategies from the last chapter, I hope you will be better equipped to head off these kinds of slumps in the future. Yet I also know all too well that long-standing behaviors, like workaholism, do not morph overnight.

Behavior change requires concerted effort. Hence the conundrum because concerted effort is the last thing you want to generate if you have gotten to the point of total overwhelm and exhaustion. Burnout is when long-term exhaustion meets diminished interest.

If you find yourself teetering on the edge of burnout, what can you do? Begin by naming the situation. Acknowledge that this is a tender and difficult place to be, especially as a leader. Burnout is not what anyone aspires to experience, much less model.

Allow and accept the accompanying emotions. There may be some tears. Carve out at least a little time and space for privacy and rest. Take a break. Even a short break can provide some relief. It could be a walk, a round of golf, reading a book, or watching a movie.

Reach out to your coach, mentor, or accountability partner. Get support. Then start prioritizing. What absolutely must get done? Write a list. Which items on the list can you possibly delegate to others, even if the tasks are a bit of a stretch for them? Star those items, then delegate.

Revisit the items you believe only you can do. What would it take to at least make an effort to move through the list, especially the important things you may have been putting off? This is not the time to dive into every little thing that is bothering you. Simply look at the big picture and begin.

Do not make yourself feel any guiltier than you already may be feeling. Stop staring into the rearview mirror and look directly in front of you. That is where you must put your attention.

Look at the clock and pledge to yourself that within one hour you simply will have started working on your list. I did not say finish your list. I said start. This is a time to be clear yet kind to yourself.

You likely will find that once you begin your list and are able to start crossing off tasks, you start feeling better about yourself and your situation. Baby steps can lead you to the path of increased productivity and renewed inspiration.

Here are some additional suggestions for getting back on a healthy, productive track and staying there:

* While you move through your to-do list, turn off notifications on your phone and computer. These are huge distractions and productivity killers. Is there anything so pressing on social media that you cannot wait to hear about later? If a truly time-sensitive e-mail comes in, the sender can pick up the phone and call you. When we hear or see a notification, it can be like an itch we suddenly need to scratch, so turn them off. I used to tell my agents that a true emergency involves blood or a bone sticking out. You can apply that here as well.

* Stop multitasking. Many studies have shown we are not as productive in any of the activities we attempt to do simultaneously as we are when we focus on just one task at a time. Women can be great multitaskers, but how does this affect overall productivity? The goal is to be truly productive, not busy. No matter what you are trying to accomplish, try to

do just one thing at time and see how much more focused you really are. Your employees and colleagues likely also will appreciate how present you are with them.

* Start moving instead of sitting all day. Even a little physical activity can be revitalizing and energizing. It can be as simple as going for a walk while on a call (even around your office if you need to refer to your computer or documents), alternating between standing and sitting while you are at your computer, or walking up and down a flight of stairs every couple of hours.

* Have you created personal boundaries? You would not miss a meeting with a client, so why not also put your extracurricular and self-care activities on your calendar? If someone asks if you can meet at that time, your answer could be, "I am sorry. I am already booked then." Then promptly propose alternate times. People like to do business with busy people, and they typically will find another time to meet.

* Learn to say no and put those things on a don't-do list.

* Take a few minutes at the end of your day to get ready for the next day. Look at your calendar and see what you need to prepare. Are there files to review or directions to check? When you put things in order the night before, you pave the way for a smoother, more productive morning.

* Practice gratitude. When you are grateful, you will feel less stressed.

* Do your best to remain positive. If you are not seeing the results you are hoping for, consider them growth opportunities. Maintain a learning mindset, and focus on the positives.

A diamond is a chunk of coal that did really well under pressure.
—Henry Kissinger

THIRTY-TWO

MANAGE SETBACKS

Henry Ford said, "Life is a series of experiences, each one of which makes us bigger, even though sometimes it is hard to realize this. For the world was built to develop character, and we must learn that the setbacks and grieves which we endure help us in our marching onward."

Setbacks refer to whatever makes you stand still, pushes you backward, or prevents you from making the progress you desire. As frustrating as these obstacles or delays can be, I encourage you to approach them as opportunities for perhaps an even bigger advance or comeback.

Resiliency refers to the tendency to recover from or adjust easily to misfortune or change. All leaders must cultivate their ability to bounce back from setbacks and move forward. How resilient are you?

Resilient people look at setbacks as opportunities to learn, grow, adapt, and be creative. They do not allow themselves to be defined or overly impacted by setbacks. They continually reassess where they have control and where they do not (e.g., the weather, the actions of a competitor, etc.), and they focus their energies toward positive ends.

Inevitably, we all will encounter situations that cause us to rethink our decisions, or are just outright mistakes. Taking those challenges and turning them into solutions is the goal.

Here are some incredible women who encountered numerous setbacks and beat the odds:

* Sandra Day O'Connor. The first female US Supreme Court Justice.

* Wilma Rudolph. At the 1960 Summer Olympics in Rome, she became the first American woman to win three gold medals in track and field during a single Olympic Games.

* Queen Elizabeth II. At sixty-five years and counting, she is the longest reigning UK monarch in history.

* Sacajawea. A Lemhi Shoshone woman who helped Lewis and Clark achieve their chartered mission objectives of exploring the Louisiana Purchase. Between 1804 and 1806 she traveled thousands of miles with the expedition from North Dakota to the Pacific Ocean, established cultural contacts with other Native Americans, and researched natural history.

By continually moving through setbacks and making incredible things happen, these are just a few women who are masters of resilience.

If you are not naturally resilient—or if you usually are but have lost your mojo—here are some ways to boost your resiliency:

* Eat well, get plenty of sleep, and manage stress through exercise. Do not take your health for granted. Taking good care of yourself will give you a better shot at being able to handle what comes your way.

* Surround yourself with motivating, inspiring people. If you cannot find an interesting gathering or conference in your area to attend, for at least the first thirty minutes of your day (which we already decided is time just for you) listen to motivational speakers or read articles or books by authors who inspire you. I realize this may be a challenge if you have young children at home. In that case, either set your alarm to get up thirty minutes before them if possible, or find another nonnegotiable thirty minutes each day to set aside for yourself.

* Learn from your mistakes and grow. There is a lesson in every situation. We all go through rough times, but I do believe, "If it doesn't kill you, it makes you stronger."

* It is not the situation that controls your journey, it is how you respond or react to it. Your reaction is always up to you.

* Make sure you set and review your goals. How else will you know whether or not you are on track?

* Build strong relationships. The more supportive your networks, personally and professionally, the more resilient you will be.

* Be flexible. Things change, plans change, people change.

* Reward yourself. Did you achieve some of your goals? Did you land a new client? Did you do something outside your comfort zone that paid off? Come up with a few rewards you are motivated to earn. They need not be expensive or outrageous. Maybe it is lunch with a girlfriend, a massage, or indulging in a special chocolate treat. What other mini rewards might inspire you?

* Find something that will bring you back to your why—and keep it nearby. It could be an article, a motivational tape, or a testimonial. For me, it is an e-mail I received from a client who described how I changed his life. That is priceless. Every time I read it, I remember why I do what I do.

Motivation, like resilience, comes from within. No one can motivate you but yourself. Remember, you need only take it one day at a time.

Remember that guy who gave up? Neither does anybody else.
—Author Unknown

THIRTY-THREE
LEARN TO FAIL

Most people don't like to talk about failure. For some, it wreaks havoc on their self-esteem. But it needn't. On the path to success, there inevitably will be hiccups along the way. Some bigger than others. How you react to the speed bumps and detours is what matters. The most important thing about failing is what it can teach you. Sometimes the lessons are obvious, and sometimes they come only through thoughtful analysis and introspection.

When faced with what I might deem a failure, two of the first questions I ask myself are "What have I learned?" and "What have I done?" Then I think and write, and write and think some more.

Here are others things I do in the face of failure, which also may be helpful to you.

1. Remind yourself that failure can accelerate success, and that YOU are not a failure. Your attempts at accomplishing something may have failed, but that is about your attempts, not you. You must separate the two. The people who don't do this are the ones who suffer major hits to their self-esteem. This can lead to unnecessary and unproductive negative spirals.

2. Take a step back and evaluate your actions. Look at everything you did and try to identify the gaps or missteps that otherwise may have led to success. If you are too close to the situation to have a clear perspective, reach out to others who may be more objective. When you ask people for their opinions about what went wrong, they may provide useful insight.

3. Seek counsel from a trusted advisor, coach, colleague, or mentor. To learn from our mistakes, we must be able to receive constructive criticism without taking it personally. Then we must apply that information to improve.

Instead of fearing failure, we should learn that failures, mistakes, errors, and setbacks provide some of the best fodder for growth.

Here are just a few examples of people who failed their way to success:

* Albert Einstein. When many people think of Albert Einstein, they immediately think "genius," but that is not the early impression he made on his parents and teachers. Einstein did not speak until he was four years old, and he did not read until he was seven. Einstein was expelled from school and was refused admittance to the Zurich Polytechnic School. He attended trade school for one year before finally being admitted to the university. He was the only one from his graduating class unable to get a teaching position because no professor would recommend him. One professor labeled him as the laziest dog he ever had in the university. The only job he initially was able to get was an entry-level position in a government patent office.

* J.K. Rowling. Rowling may be seen as a true success story with her Harry Potter series, but before that she was nearly penniless, divorced, and trying to raise a child on her own while attending school and writing a novel. Through hard work and determination, Rowling went from depending on welfare to being one of the richest women in the world in a span of only five years. Reflecting on her failures, she has said, "It is impossible to live without failing at something, unless you live so cautiously that you might as well not have lived at all—in which case, you fail by default."

* Thomas Edison. In his early years, teachers told Edison he was "too stupid to learn anything." He fared no better at work and was fired from his first two jobs for not being productive enough. Even as an inventor, Edison made one thousand unsuccessful attempts before inventing the light bulb. When asked how he felt about failing one thousand times, he purportedly said that he had not failed and rather, "The light bulb was an invention with one thousand steps."

* Michael Jordan. This all-time basketball great was cut from his high school basketball team. Jordan did not let this setback stop him from playing the game he loved. He has famously stated, "I have missed more than 9,000 shots in my career. I have lost almost 300 games. On 26 occasions I have been entrusted to take the game-winning shot, and I missed. I have failed over and over and over again in my life. And that's precisely why I succeed."

Building on Michael Jordan's statement that repeated failures can pave the way for success, here is additional food for thought.

1. Failures can be a precursor to career success. Did you know that many companies actually look for CEOs who previously have failed? Failures come with the opportunity to carefully assess what went wrong and determine changes that can be made moving forward. When leaders can admit they are human and that they messed up—and, moreover, that they are genuinely all the wiser for it—their credibility goes up.

2. The willingness to make mistakes can lead to excellence. Some people refer to this as their "growth mindset," and they proactively develop their talents and abilities. This takes dedication and mentoring, and those with this mindset seek challenges to accelerate their continued learning and growth.

3. Innovation requires experimentation. You cannot avoid risk if you value creativity and innovation. Creativity requires risk, and risk often leads to failure. It is not the flops that count, but what you do after the flops.

Remember FAIL need not always have a negative connotation. Another way to look at the word is First Attempt In Learning.

It is not the challenge that will change you; it is the way you choose to respond to it.

Success is going from failure to failure without loss of enthusiasm.
—Winston Churchill

PART 7

GENEROSITY

When you imagine what generosity looks like, what images come to mind? Children sharing toys or snacks? People donating money to a cause? Groups coming together to support families in need? These are wonderful examples, and I have been fortunate to participate in all of these. But my absolute favorite thing to donate happens to be my most valuable possession ... my time.

I love sharing my experiences and expertise with others. Sometimes they do not have any other resources, and I might say or do that one thing that changes their life. I often readily volunteer to do what needs to be done if no one else steps up to the plate. Occasionally I am criticized for being too available—typically by well-meaning people who say I dilute my brand by giving my material away for free.

However, I don't consider these transactions to be "free" because the recipients must also use their most valuable possession, their time. For me, it is all about the Golden Rule. Do unto others as you would have them do unto you.

I recently asked the audience members at an event if they lived by the Golden Rule. Some raised their hands but many didn't. I then asked if they knew what the Golden Rule was, and again some raised their hands but many didn't. When I defined it and asked who had ever experienced it, everyone's hands went up. Maybe generosity needs to be brought back into fashion. As with everything, education and reminders are important.

Being generous is about giving without any expectations of receiving. However, being generous also means you are able to receive. How many times have you given someone a compliment and the person looked at you and either said nothing, looked shocked, or began to explain why what you said isn't really so?

Today there are many companies and businesses that exemplify corporate and community responsibility by giving back and donating. It helps that more and more people are prioritizing doing business with companies that are philanthropic.

Consider what your business or employer stands for and who your market is. Are they well matched? Moreover, does the business consistently operate in accordance with its stated values, and do those values align with yours?

It is deeply rewarding to give something great to your clients as well as the larger community. There is much good to be done in the world, and all of us can contribute.

Generosity soaks everyone with its wonderful energy.
—Author Unknown

THIRTY-FOUR
SERVANT LEADERSHIP

Has this happened to you? You are conducting business as you always have—listening, caring, and being empathetic—when you learn there is a special name for what you do every day? A phrase that, soon thereafter, you hear being bandied about seemingly everywhere? That was my introduction to the term "servant leadership."

Although the principles of servant leadership are timeless, it was seven or so years ago that I first heard the now ubiquitous term. I was in a one-on-one meeting with someone I met at a networking event. She was telling me how she just revamped her business because she decided she wanted to be a servant-leader. I thought she was speaking another language and asked her what that was. She was shocked I didn't know what she was referring to, and she began to counsel me on what it meant to serve others.

I started to giggle and told her I have done that my entire life. I just didn't know it had a special name. After that brief encounter, maybe because I giggled at the term, it suddenly seemed that every other person was now labeling themself as a servant-leader.

I had a conversation about this with my husband. As a retired Air Force Colonel, servant leadership is a big part of who he is. He told me that true leaders always serve others. In the military his job was to develop and take care of his team emotionally, professionally, personally, and physically. He also had to make sure he steered his team away from unnecessary risk. As the person in charge, he had to develop emerging leaders who ultimately would surpass his skills and fill his place.

This is something that we as leaders do all the time ... don't we? If we don't, we should. There is a big difference between leaders and managers. As a manager you manage things, and as a leader you lead people.

I have often wondered why there are any examples of women not wanting to help other women. A great leader should not be threatened by anyone who comes into her department or company. To the contrary, she should want to support and promote the newcomers. This is in the best interests of the organization as a whole and the individuals who comprise it.

As someone who practiced servant leadership before it was in vogue, I have gladly promoted myself right out of my position on numerous occasions while preparing the next generation of leaders to take their places.

Being a servant-leader has many faces. Sometimes it means lending an ear to listen or a shoulder to cry on. Believe it or not, that is huge for some people. It can also entail putting others before you and your desires. In other situations, it involves inspiring others when they need it most. No matter the circumstance, being a servant-leader requires that you lead with your team in mind. You are not in competition with your team. You are not more interested in managing up than managing down. You are making sure that what your team needs is what you bring to the table.

I have always said that if I could freely give all of my professional time to young women starting out in business and guide them through the maze of craziness they are sure to encounter, I would do it in a second. To do so, I would have to convince the bank that my mortgage could wait or the utility company that they could let my payments slide. I would love to be able to lead without being in a leadership role with a leadership title. I would do it because that is what I truly believe will help not only the next generation of women, but our economy and society and world ... in a small but meaningful way.

Since that is not my current reality, I do what I can. When I speak to a group of women, I occasionally will ask what they think can happen in fifteen minutes of time. Some might say they could have "a fast glass of wine" or "a quick bite to eat." Then I ask them what they think can be accomplished in fifteen minutes of business time. Responses include "respond to a few e-mails" or "have a quick conversation."

My next question is, "What do you think I can see in your business in fifteen minutes that might uncover a challenge we can work through together?" I offer as many women in the room as I have time to accommodate, a fifteen-minute, laser-focused session. In that time, we discuss their number one challenge, and I freely offer ideas or suggestions about how to approach it.

People always ask why I do that. It's simple. If someone gave me fifteen minutes of their undivided attention to support me earlier in my career, I would have learned so much and my path might have been different. I put myself in their shoes every single time.

While the idea of servant leadership goes back thousands of years, the modern servant leadership movement was launched by Robert C. Greenleaf in 1970 when he published his essay, "The Servant as Leader," and coined the terms "servant-leader" and "servant leadership." By then, Greenleaf had already spent half a century working to shape large institutions.

After carefully considering Greenleaf's extensive writing on the subject, Larry C. Spears, Servant-Leadership Scholar, Gonzaga University and President & CEO, The Spears Center for Servant-Leadership (2008-Present); and, Former President and CEO of the Robert K. Greenleaf Center for Servant Leadership (1990-2007), extracted the following ten core characteristics of servant leadership. These originally appeared in the book, *Practicing Servant Leadership*, and were adapted in his essay, "The Understanding and Practice of Servant Leadership."

How many of the qualities from the slightly edited version of his excerpt do you recognize in yourself?

1. Listening. Leaders have traditionally been valued for their communication and decision-making skills. While these are also important skills for the servant-leader, they need to be reinforced by a deep commitment to listening intently to others. The servant-leader seeks to identify the will of a group and helps clarify that will. He or she seeks to listen receptively to what is being said (and not said!). Listening

also encompasses getting in touch with one's own inner voice and seeking to understand what one's body, spirit, and mind are communicating. Listening, coupled with regular periods of reflection, is essential to the growth of the servant-leader.

2. Empathy. The servant-leader strives to understand and empathize with others. People need to be accepted and recognized for their special and unique spirits. One assumes the good intentions of coworkers and does not reject them as people, even while refusing to accept their behavior or performance. The most successful servant-leaders are those who have become skilled empathetic listeners.

3. Healing. Learning to heal is a powerful force for transformation and integration. One of the great strengths of servant leadership is the potential for healing oneself and others. Many people have broken spirits and have suffered from a variety of emotional hurts. Although this is a part of being human, servant-leaders recognize that they have an opportunity to "help make whole" those with whom they come in contact.

4. Awareness. General awareness, and especially self-awareness, strengthens the servant-leader. Making a commitment to foster awareness can be scary—you never know what you may discover. Awareness also aids one in understanding issues involving ethics and values. It lends itself to being able to view most situations from a more integrated, holistic position.

5. Persuasion. Another characteristic of servant-leaders is a primary reliance on persuasion, rather than using one's positional authority, in making decisions within an organization.

The servant-leader seeks to convince others rather than coerce compliance. This particular element offers one of the clearest distinctions between the traditional authoritarian model and that of servant leadership. The servant-leader is effective at building consensus within groups.

6. Conceptualization. Servant-leaders seek to nurture their abilities to "dream great dreams." The ability to look at a problem or organization from a conceptualizing perspective means that one must think beyond day-to-day realities. For many managers this is a characteristic that requires discipline and practice. The traditional manager is focused on the need to achieve short-term operational goals. The manager who wishes to also be a servant-leader must stretch his or her thinking to encompass broader based conceptual thinking.

7. Foresight. Foresight is a characteristic that enables the servant-leader to understand the lessons from the past, the realities of the present, and the likely consequence of a decision for the future. It is also deeply rooted within the intuitive mind. As such, one can conjecture that foresight is the one servant-leader characteristic with which one may be born. All other characteristics can be consciously developed.

8. Stewardship. Robert Greenleaf's view of all institutions was one in which CEOs, staffs, and trustees all played significant roles in holding their institutions in trust for the greater good of society. Servant leadership, like stewardship, assumes first and foremost a commitment to serving the needs of others. It also emphasizes the use of openness and persuasion rather than control.

9. Commitment to the growth of people. Servant-leaders believe that people have an intrinsic value beyond their tangible contributions as workers. As such, the servant-leader is deeply committed to the growth of each and every individual within his or her institution. The servant-leader recognizes the tremendous responsibility to do everything within his or her power to nurture the personal, professional, and spiritual growth of employees. This can include, but is not limited to, concrete actions such as making available funds for personal and professional development, taking a personal interest in others' ideas and suggestions, encouraging worker involvement in decision-making, and actively assisting laid-off workers to find other employment.

10. Building community. The servant-leader senses that much has been lost in recent human history as a result of the shift from local communities to large institutions as the primary shaper of human lives. This awareness causes the servant-leader to seek to identify some means for building community among those who work within a given institution.

Whether you are in a corporate position or in an entrepreneurial venture, being a servant-leader is definitely a role you want to inhabit.

The servant-leader is servant first. It begins with the natural feeling that one wants to serve. Then conscious choice brings one to aspire to lead. The best test is: do those served grow as persons; do they, while being served, become healthier, wiser, freer, more autonomous, more likely themselves to become servants?
—Robert K. Greenleaf

THIRTY-FIVE

SERVE OTHERS

The most successful people in this world genuinely want to help others.

Here are a few ways you might consider being of service.

1. Find out what is most valuable to the person you want to help. To truly help someone and make a difference, you need to be crystal clear about how to accomplish that. Want to know the easiest way to find out? Ask them! You can simply say, "How can I help you?" or "How can I serve you best?" Of course you must mean it—then deliver. It doesn't matter if you don't equally value what they need because you are seeking to learn what is valuable to *them*.

2. Give your time. Many people believe they must open their wallets to help others. In truth, what others might most need is another great asset of yours ... your time. Be discerning when you give this resource. You will want the recipient to value your time as much as you do.

3. Share knowledge. As an expert in your field, you have knowledge that can change someone's life. You may have experienced struggles they are encountering now or will face in the future. Don't be afraid to share. Being a life changer is a great title to wear.

4. Share resources. When you meet someone and are nurturing the relationship, you may have the impulse to help them build their business. Scroll through your contacts and offer a resource or two. It doesn't have to lead to a million-dollar contract, but it may be someone who can make their lives a little easier like a virtual assistant, an IT person, an accountant, or an attorney. If these service providers come with a seal of approval from you, it can be quite useful.

5. Create opportunities. You know the old saying, "When opportunity knocks, open the door"? Well some people don't easily notice opportunities. The second part of that quote is, "And if there isn't a door, build one." You can serve others by being the architect that builds the door for them. Perhaps it looks like an introduction, a speaking gig, or so much more.

Good, strong business leaders are more influential than they may realize.

Here are more tenets of servant leadership:

* Lead. Lead by example and respect others. Do not expect anyone to work harder than you.

* Teach. Make sure everyone you work with gets to experience some of your brilliance. You don't have to do a brain dump. A little can go a long way.

* Inspire. Everyone benefits from being inspired and motivated. Find out what people need to keep them moving in the right direction, and help them access it. Respect is earned, and it goes both ways.

* Mentor. Think about what you wanted when you were coming through the ranks or decided to open your business. Share your experience and your expertise. Hold your mentee accountable, and make sure you love them when they need it.

* Serve. Your success is dependent on your actions. When you consistently serve others with your product, service, knowledge, and experience, you will take your business to another level. You will attract the right people to work with you and become raving fans. Who wouldn't want to be around a business or person who thinks more about others than they do about themselves?

I now would like to broaden the scope of what it means to pay it forward by moving beyond the workplace and our daily interactions with other adults. Let's turn our attention to how we can teach our children about serving others. Giving and receiving are the cycle of life, and it is never too early to begin conveying this important lesson.

Here are some ways you can teach your children or other young people the concept of service in a way that is enjoyable for them:

* Start by letting them work alongside you. You must lead by example and teach as you go. As you proceed through your tasks, teach a little and move along. With each new activity, the young ones are observing your skills and acts of service. When you add stories about why you do things in a certain way, you provide more for them to store in their expanding memory banks.

* Teach your children to notice what needs to be done. For example, we may take it for granted that our children should know that the water glass shouldn't be close to the edge of the table. But why should we assume they will visualize the glass being knocked over and shattering on the floor, especially if they have not witnessed that before? Take a moment to point out why it is a good idea to move the glass. As another example, when your child wants a snack, ask them if they think their sibling might like one as well. It is a gentle way to get them in the habit of thinking about and caring for others.

* Let them know it is okay to ask, "What can I do for you?" instead of waiting to be told what to do. A big hug goes a long way when they ask.

* Give them time to learn. Serving is not always natural behavior. It comes more easily for some people than for others. It may take time before you see evidence of your children's desire to serve, but trust they are learning and experiencing benefits from their efforts. With continued encouragement and guidance, you will see results, as your children become young adults you can be proud of every single day.

In teaching others, we teach ourselves.

Success has nothing to do with what you gain in life or accomplish for yourself. It's what you do for others.
—Danny Thomas

THIRTY-SIX

GIVE BACK

Another way to give back dropped into my lap during a recent holiday season. Between the Colonel and me, we have four children. They are pretty good about letting us know what they would like to receive for the holidays, and we are pretty good about fulfilling their requests. This particular year was different.

When I reached out to ask what was on their wish lists, my daughter said she didn't want us to get her a gift. Instead, she requested we donate the money we otherwise would have spent on her to her friend's family whose five-year-old son was undergoing chemotherapy. During this extremely stressful time for that family, my daughter wanted to do what she could to ease their financial burden. Inspired by my daughter's request, we not only contributed money in her name to the family in need, but we similarly gifted our other three children by donating their gift money to causes of their choosing.

During the holidays many people donate their time to soup kitchens and shelters. These are wonderful ways of giving back. What about during the rest of the year? Many shelters and soup kitchens need help year-round, as do dozens of other community organizations.

How do you regularly give to causes greater than yourself? In some respects this takes us back to our first section on passion where I posed questions like, "Beyond work or your business or career, what really lights you up?" If you are an animal lover, for example, you might enjoy volunteering for your local humane society. Perhaps teaching people to read is more your speed. Or, you might prefer to dedicate energy to social or humanitarian causes. The possibilities are endless.

Here are a handful of other ideas:

* Donate clothing, furniture, and other possessions to those in need.

* Raise money by participating in sponsored bike-a-thons, runs, or walks.

* If you aren't physically able to participate in these athletic events, volunteer to help on the day of the event at registration tables or at the food, drink, or First Aid stations.

* Teach English as a second language as a literacy volunteer, or as a first language to kids or adults who need help.

* Tutor children in math or another subject.

* Remove trash from rivers or streams in your area.

Doing community service with your family and friends is a wonderful way to spend time together. Volunteering is good for your health and happiness. Studies have shown that people who volunteer live longer. Volunteering is also a terrific tool in the fight against depression because it can be easier to temporarily forget about your own problems when you shift your focus to helping others.

When you commit to something bigger than yourself, you are tapping into a vision that inspires you. Additionally, you are working with other like-minded people, either in person or virtually. The act of committing to something beyond you, your business, and your immediate family can help fill you up and generate enthusiasm you can channel into being a transformational leader.

To give back, pay it forward, or otherwise contribute to something beyond your daily life, you must intend to give without any expectation of receiving. It has been said that real generosity is doing something for someone who could never pay you back.

Here is a recent, funny example. I was on a flight from Dallas to Fort Lauderdale, and the entire North Texas Mean Green men's basketball team and coaches were on my flight. The young men were polite, intelligent, and extremely tall. I was seated next to the team captain, and as we waited for everyone to board, we chatted about his goals and plans for the future. As we were talking, another player was walking up and down the aisle trying to get a teammate to swap seats because he could not get his long legs into the seat he was assigned. They all struggled with the legroom.

Observing this, I asked where he was sitting and offered to trade seats with him because I was in the emergency row. Due to my height constraints, legroom is not of great importance to me. He was so appreciative. My new seat was next to one of the coaches, and we chatted for most of the flight.

Paying it forward comes in various forms. It didn't even occur to me that my one small gesture could change someone's day. But seeing his beaming face as we got off the plane (then taking a picture together) confirmed that's exactly what I had done. You can't put a price on that. By the way, he is seven feet tall. I am five foot two.

Here are simple ways to be generous in everyday life:

* Anonymously give money you can spare to someone who needs it.

* Listen fully to someone's story without feeling the need to one-up them or tell your own.

* Let someone vent, even if you can't offer a solution, without considering how well (or not) they did the same for you last week.

* Ask, "What can I do to help you today?" Then follow through. Do not keep track of your good deeds. You are serving simply for the sake of serving.

* Let someone else educate you, even if you are tempted to stay closed-minded. Then let them know you appreciate their willingness to share their knowledge.

* To demonstrate respect, give your full attention to the person speaking to you even if you are tempted to let your thoughts wander.

* Accompany someone to an appointment or drive them to an interview so they feel strong and supported.

* Leave a thoughtful comment on someone's blog, not to promote yourself but rather to show them how they positively affected you.

* Tell someone you believe in their potential (if you do), even if they have not always shown you the same support.

In the wise and timeless words of Anne Frank, "No one has ever become poor from giving."

Now, what can you do through work? If you work at a large company, see if there are community service projects, volunteer opportunities, or if they will match your donations to charities.

If you work at a smaller company or are an entrepreneur, here are some ways to give back to your community:

* Promote local businesses. One of the best ways to support your community is to patronize other businesses in the area. Buy local as often possible. Share links to your favorite local companies on social media. This also can be a way for you to locate strategic partners—people or businesses whose services complement rather than compete with yours. Consider the wonderful partnerships you can create. There is always strength in numbers.

* Sponsor a youth sports team. Chances are that one of your coworkers or business colleagues has a child on a youth sports team. By finding a local team to sponsor, you can help

with the team's funding while getting publicity in exchange for your support. This is a simple way to lend support with very minimal time investment.

* Hold a contest. You can contribute to your community while also encouraging others to have fun by holding a contest. Choose a local charity, and instead of prizes, funds raised will go to that charity. Another approach is to structure the contest so that funds raised go to charities chosen by the winners.

* Offer your skills. As a leader in your industry, you have valuable expertise that can benefit others. If you are a business owner, consider teaching classes on entrepreneurship to local residents. If you are a leader in the corporate sector, offer to teach a specialized skill needed by those returning to the workforce or changing career paths.

You likely will need to set boundaries. Otherwise you may find yourself giving so much that you have no time for yourself. Like everything else, take out your calendar and schedule the time you can give to others. Be realistic and don't overcommit.

When I find myself being pulled in too many directions, I make a list of everything my hands are touching. Then I assess what must stay and what needs to be considered for release. While this is not always easy to do, managing my time well is what enables me to be present and available for what I most value in all aspects of my life.

The results of philanthropy are always beyond calculation.
—Miriam Beard

THIRTY-SEVEN
PAY IT FORWARD AS A MENTOR

One of my greatest joys is giving with the pure intention of giving by paying it forward. Now make no mistake, my company is a for-profit company and I have bills to pay like everyone else, but I always make time to pay it forward and mentor young women.

For much of my career, I was either the only woman or one of the only women in the room. I launched my company, Selling In A Skirt, to support women, particularly those working in male-dominated fields. I wanted to show women how to succeed in business without sacrificing their values or attributes. I wanted them to understand we inherently have amazing feminine qualities that can propel us forward in business ... if we use them correctly.

While mentoring young women naturally complements my work at Selling In A Skirt, I mentored women for many years before launching this business. Each of the young women I have mentored throughout my career just needed a little help. Some may have needed it for a longer period of time than others, but in truth, what they all most needed was someone who cared. Someone to help them get a leg up without judging their mistakes, and someone who believed in them when maybe they felt like no one else did.

My friend and corporate gender strategist, Jeffery Tobias Halter, reminds me how valuable it can be for women to mentor men and for men to mentor women. Throughout his business experience in sales and most recently in corporate gender equity, Jeffery has seen firsthand how the cross-pollination of ideas helps break down gender stereotypes, perceived norms, and unconscious gender bias.

A mentor offers perspective, insight, and encouragement. Mentors give their mentees the benefit of their education and experience to help develop the mentees' skills and abilities.

Both parties need to want to be in this partnership and must feel free to ask each other questions and challenge one another. By no means is it necessary that they agree on everything.

This is how we all learn, and each relationship is unique. If you have mentored more than one person, you know firsthand how different each mentoring experience can be. Ideally your mentee will go on to mentor someone else, and the cycle of paying it forward will continue. Mentors learn more than they might expect, and the experience is priceless.

If you are an emerging leader, why might you seek a mentor? Here are a few reasons.

1. Mentors have been there and done that. You can learn from your mentor's mistakes as well as their successes.

2. You can talk to someone who is nonjudgmental and has no preconceived notions about you. They see you for you. I see potential in all my mentees that they may not yet see in themselves.

3. Mentors generally have a valuable network of business contacts they might introduce you to when the time is right. While you might otherwise meet and connect with some of these people on your own, your mentor may be able to condense that timeline.

4. The relationship is priceless. The experience is invaluable.

5. Open, honest discussions with your mentor may uncover new areas of interest. You may even discover that your passion and purpose emerge from what now feels like clutter in your brain.

On the other side of the equation, why might you want to be a mentor? Beyond what I already have mentioned, here are a few additional benefits.

1. Being a mentor can help you with generational challenges. Since you typically will be working with someone younger than you, it can provide up close insight into a professional of that age, which might help bridge generation gaps in various parts of your life.

2. Being a mentor can help you redefine your own career path and goals. Many times as you share information and experience, you may ask yourself why you aren't doing what you advise your mentee to do.

3. Even though you might have begun working decades ago, do you remember how it felt to be the new kid on the block? It can be deeply gratifying to help orient someone else and provide them with a road map for a smoother journey.

4. You can have a positive, tremendous impact on some-one's life. Mentoring is a significant responsibility. Do you know how it feels when a former mentee tells you how you changed their life? This may not happen right away. It could be years later when they remind you of a thought, phrase, or idea you shared. You may never know the full effects of your efforts.

Let's say you have decided you would like to become a men-tor. Congratulations! Here are a few tips on being the best mentor you can be.

1. Approach each mentee and mentoring relationship as if it is unique, because it is. Prepare questions to ask yourself as well as your mentee(s). Here are some possibilities: What are your expectations? How will you communicate so that it is optimal for both parties? How will you measure success? How will you make the time together beneficial and safe?

2. Think about what you would have liked or did like when you were in a position similar to your mentee's. As you refresh your memory, also allow yourself to be informed by what did not work for you.

3. Be interested in your mentee as a person, not as another job. This relationship is very personal and valuable. Get to know them and what makes them who they are. You do not have to be best friends, but you also do not want to be so clinical that it feels as if you are a doctor and they are the patient. Ask a lot of questions and show you are actively listening. Sure, it is important to learn more about their desired career path and what they are struggling with, but it also can be meaningful to hear about that championship

football game from the past weekend or the concert they have been looking forward to for months. Many senior leaders struggle with work-life balance. Your mentee might be able to shed some light on that for you.

4. Do not be too quick to advise your mentee with the hopes you will appear to be a prophetic knight in shining armor. Get all the details regarding their current situation, ask more questions, and consider various possible courses of action for your mentee. Just as you would do when you have a big decision to make for your business, take time to review the information before advising. By the way, demonstrating how you take time to consider and try to fully understand what may be at stake is also a valuable lesson for your mentee.

5. With that said, do not assume anything about your mentee. Just because they are a certain gender, generation, or ethnicity, does not mean they fit stereotypes. This is where even more questions can deliver valuable information. Even if think you've been there and done that, remember that the circumstances, times, and people involved are different. Ask, listen, and then offer your feedback. We all know what happens when we assume, right?

6. Be real with your mentee. It is fine, in fact it's healthy, to let them know you are not perfect. As appropriate, share some of your past mistakes or failures. For example, I was devastated when I did not pass my first insurance exam. When I share that with my mentees, they tend to appreciate my honesty and vulnerability. Plus they can see that that one little setback, although it seemed monumental to me at the time, was truly just a hiccup and a lesson.

7. Acknowledge and celebrate your mentee's achievements and milestones. This can boost their motivation and confidence, and help keep them focused.

8. Lead by example. Remember you are their role model. They are watching you even when you don't think they are. You cannot simply say you have a strong work ethic or high integrity ... you must live it. Being a mentor keeps you at your best.

Life's deepest rewards come from helping others and expecting nothing in return. If you truly can release expectations, you might be surprised by what comes your way.

Generosity is a magical cycle.

If you light a lamp for someone,
it will also brighten your own path.
—Author Unknown

NEXT STEPS

When I reflect upon this book and the Walking on the Glass Floor Foundation, I return to where I began so many years ago. In the Introduction, I shared my story about the first time I heard, "Girls don't do things like this!" It was my father's stern admonishment that led me to where I am today.

I am a firm believer in equality and opportunity. My company's tagline is, "Women want to be treated equally, not identically. ™"

While I am encouraged by the many opportunities women have today that were not even on my radar when I was growing up, we still have a ways to go when it comes to women in leadership positions. Plenty of people discuss statistics and debate what could have, should have, and might have been.

But the reality is that even though women are not yet represented in positions of leadership at nearly the scale we should be, many women are successfully advancing toward and into leadership roles. Often with the help of other women. Our job is to keep them there and lend additional support. I always say that recruiting is easy; retention is the hard part.

Walking on the glass floor is a readily accessible visual. Having moved beyond the ceiling, you are now walking on the glass floor. I envision a growing movement of women talking about this glass floor—the flip side of the glass ceiling—while being supported to continually learn and grow as leaders.

Through the Walking on the Glass Floor Foundation, we are bringing together subject matter experts and women in leadership to mastermind about continuing to improve the business landscape. We are mentoring women new to the "floor" and helping emerging leaders reach the first rung on the ladder and continue on up. We are curating a collection of books and other resources created by fellow women thought leaders who have been there, done that, and proudly wear the T-shirt—as well as those by some amazing men committed to women's leadership.

The foundation is about inclusion and diversity. It isn't about leaving men out. It's about inviting and welcoming their support to this wonderful world of women in leadership. It's also about women expanding upon and developing their own networks.

If just one senior woman had reached out and taken me by the hand to show me the ropes when I was starting in business, I can only imagine how much smoother my journey would have been. In the 1970s in sales in the companies that employed me, there simply were no women in leadership positions. The only women on my path of advancement were me, myself, and I.

I created the foundation to fill the void I experienced. My sincere hope is that women will experience the Walking on the Glass Floor Foundation as a place that guides and supports them with their leadership goals. As a forum that introduces them to people, ideas, concepts, and tools to which they might not otherwise have had access. And, that it be a rich resource for women leaders at every stage of their careers.

You are not alone. As Glinda the Good Witch said, "You had the power all along." Let the Walking on the Glass Floor Foundation be your ruby slippers.

ABOUT THE AUTHORS

JUDY HOBERMAN

Judy Hoberman is Executive Director of the Walking on the Glass Floor Foundation and President of Selling In A Skirt. She has created a suite of workshops, seminars, and coaching programs that take the negativity out of selling. Her thirty years in sales have given her knowledge of and a sense of humor about gender differences in the workplace. Judy's humorous stories about how men and women sell, manage, recruit, and supervise differently shed light on how both genders can better support each other's successes.

As Executive Director of the Walking on the Glass Floor Foundation, Judy has the honor and privilege of supporting companies and organizations that include "women in leadership" in their vision—as well as the women they serve! She helps identify and target industries and individuals to join forces with to create an environment where women in leadership thrive. Beyond thriving, they give back in various ways, including but not limited to extending a hand to other women to make their journeys less challenging and lonely.

Judy is an award-winning Corporate Training Director with extensive experience in training, course development, and project management. She was personally selected by the President and CEO of a large insurance company to relocate to Dallas to bring her talents in training to their corporate headquarters as well as to one hundred field offices in forty-four states. In that role, Judy taught more than three thousand agents how to decipher the mysteries of the sales process and create authentic selling systems. In turn, the field agents awarded her with their Character and Integrity Award for her distinct and significant contributions to their successes.

Judy also was named by the Women of Visionary Influence as a finalist for their Mentor of the Year award. She regularly works with companies to improve diversity and women's initiatives in the areas of recruiting, training, coaching, mentoring, and retention.

Prior to *Walking on the Glass Floor: Seven Essential Qualities of Women Who Lead*, Judy authored three business books for professional women, sales executives, and entrepreneurs. Her previous books are *Selling In A Skirt, Famous Isn't Enough*, and *Pure Wealth*.

She hosts a weekly radio show on The Women 4 Women Network/iHeart Radio called Selling In A Skirt and is featured as "The Gender Expert" on Fox News Radio. Judy has appeared on CNN Headlines, ABC, CBS, CW33, and Good Morning Texas, and has contributed articles to numerous publications and journals. She has appeared on the cover of *Exceptional People Magazine* and is a frequent public speaker. In 2016 she gave a very well-received TEDx Talk about the impacts of pre-judging people.

Judy's mission is to help women live her SKIRT philosophy—Standing Out, Keys to Success, Inspiration, Results, and Time Management—all while having fun.

STACEY STERN

Stacey Stern is a communication consultant and writer who works with inspired change makers. She loves helping people access and articulate the clearest, truest vision of themselves and their organizations.

Stacey guides businesses and foundations to raise the bar with their internal and external communications. She also partners with dynamic leaders to coauthor books about personal and professional growth.

More high energy than Zen personality-wise, Stacey is authentic to the core and brings her heart, mind, and integrity wherever she goes. www.staceystern.com

WALKING ON THE
GLASS FLOOR PRESS

Walking on the Glass Floor Press is dedicated to sourcing, publishing, and distributing educational materials for women in leadership and organizations that support women in leadership.

To order books, visit our online store at:
www.walkingontheglassfloor.com

Special discounts on bulk quantities are available to businesses, non-profit organizations, book clubs, and women's groups.

If you are inspired to become involved with the Walking on the Glass Floor Foundation, please e-mail Judy at:
judy@walkingontheglassfloor.com

To contact Judy about speaking engagements or coaching, please e-mail her at:
judy@walkingontheglassfloor.com

Made in the USA
Middletown, DE
19 June 2019